Economic
Transformation
the Mexican Way

The Lionel Robbins Lectures

Economic Transformation the Mexican Way

Pedro Aspe

The MIT Press
Cambridge, Massachusetts
London, England

This book was set in Palatino by DEKR Corporation, Woburn, MA and printed and bound by Maple-Vail, Inc. in the United States of America.

Library of Congress Cataloging-in-Publication Data

Aspe Armella, Pedro.
  Economic transformation the Mexican way / Pedro Aspe.
    p. cm.—(The Lionel Robbins lectures)
  Includes bibliographical references and index.
  ISBN 0-262-01135-2
  1. Mexico—Economic policy—1970–   2. Fiscal policy—Mexico.
3. Economic stabilization—Mexico. I. Title. II. Series.
HC 135.A8328   1993
338.972—dc20   93-19949
                                                     CIP

To Concha

To Sofía, Mónica, Pedro, and Carlos

hoping they will live in a fairer
and more prosperous Mexico

Contents

Preface

On Christmas Eve 1990 I received a very pleasant albeit unexpected call. On the other end of the line was my good friend Richard Layard, who was eager to break some exciting news: an invitation from the Lionel Robbins committee to be its lecturer for 1992. When we finished our conversation, I was not only thrilled by the honor of this distinction, but also especially moved by the memories of the impact that the writings of Professor Robbins have had throughout my career as an economics student, a teacher, and a public servant.

I have to go back to the very beginning of my experience as an economist to trace the history of what I learned from the ideas of Mr. Robbins. It was during my first course in political economy that I read his *Theory of Economic Policy*. Thereafter I think I must have read every work that came from his fertile pen: *The Economist in the Twentieth Century, Autobiography of an Economist, An Essay on the Nature and Significance of Economic Science,* and the vast succession of articles, both constructive and controversial, which he contributed to various professional and other journals.

In many ways I think that Professor Robbins is one of the most prescient economists of our time. His vision of the role of the state and economic policy on economic growth and the well-being of society foresaw most of the rapid, changes that we are now witnessing in every country of the world. Almost half a century ago, when the debate between Keynesian and classical economics seemed to divide the options for market economies into either a strong government presence in every area of the economy or the unrestricted predominance of market over social needs, Robbins was the only one to come out with what economic experience is proving to be the most pragmatic and responsible definition of the role of economic policy in economic development.

He rightly said that it was not for the state to intervene where markets can do better in terms of resource allocation and distribution of income; but he also stated that it was equally unwise to forego the capacity of the state to regulate when markets fail to grant equal access to every individual or remain blind to the realities of poverty and marginalization. As economic policy has been catching up with the reality of our time, the ideas of the great political economists like Robbins acquire a new social dimension and inspire people everywhere to produce greater fairness and wealth within their societies.

Almost nine years ago, Mexico chose the road to modernization. At a time when we were immersed in the confusion of an economic crisis and deceived by the mirage of our paternalistic state, we had to look again at the fundamentals. We had to define the way in which the productive forces of our country should be reorganized to produce goods and services and bring the benefits of growth to all members of society.

Maybe the reason I was so touched by the candid and yet profound explanations of Professor Robbins when I first read him has to do with the contradictions I found between the national project for Mexico, as established in our Constitution, and the way in which we as a country were trying to get there. Our stated objective is to remain a sovereign nation, capable of deciding how to define its role among the other nations of the world. We responded to the call for sovereignty by isolating ourselves from new ideas instead of seeing that sovereignty is achieved through innovation, imagination, competition, and cooperation in an integrated world.

The constitutional aim of Mexico is a democratic one achieved not only through free access to the polls and freedom of speech, but also through the right to an education, to a job, to a fair salary, to do business, to health, to an adequate pension, to decent housing and other basic needs. Our failure in carrying out this mandate lay in thinking that the state on its own had to provide everything, without respect for the initiatives and creativity of individuals.

Modernization as it is taking place in Mexico is not an abstract concept for academic debate; rather it has a profound social dimension. It is the commitment to respect the initiatives of the community and to promote individual achievement; it is based on the inevitable need to increase the importance of the citizen and better organize the building and running of the state. It is aimed at strengthening Mexico through unity, progress, and social justice. My generation was educated in a context where the greater presence of the state was thought of as synonymous with more social justice. For many years, when it was necessary to promote the industrialization of the country, the state created enterprises and public entities to channel resources and subsidies. It bought companies in financial difficulties to save jobs and to support production.

From the evidence provided by the years of crisis, we can now say that these were not always the right decisions. We know that a bigger state is not necessarily a more capable state. In reality, in the case of Mexico, more state meant a diminished ability to respond to the social needs of our fellow countrymen, and in the end, a weaker state. While the productive activity of the public sector increased, attention to the problems of drinking water, health, investment in agriculture, nutrition, housing, environment, and justice deteriorated very rapidly. The stabilization of the economy through realistic budget management, the privatization of state-owned enterprises, fiscal reform, economic deregulation, financial reform, the liberalization of trade, the renegotation of the external debt, and the strengthening of land tenure rights is the new way in which the people of Mexico are carrying out an ambitious reform of the state. We are facing the challege of making the transition to an open economy and an open society. In abandoning its role of proprietor, the state has taken on greater solidarity with the needs of the poor.

I have had the great opportunity of living through a period of extensive change in the economic history of Mexico, and it has been my good fortune to observe some of it from favorable positions. The purpose of this book is to provide a straightforward account of the way in which Mexico has been going through this transition.

As I understand it, Lionel Robbins used to tell anyone doing research with him that while the description of economic policy at a given time can help us to see how the different elements of society interact, it is only through economic history that one can understand why these relationships exist the way they do. Following this valuable remark, I decided to prepare these lectures by looking at the recent developments in Mexico from a long-run perspective, especially as regards structural change.

In the first lecture I talk about the macroeconomic stabilization experience of Mexico, placing special emphasis on its social and political aspects. The success already achieved in terms of stabilization, production, and employment, especially during the last four years, has been as much the result of fiscal and monetary discipline as of the orderly negotiation and consensus of workers, farmers, entrepreneurs, and the government through the existing institutional channels.

In the second lecture (chapters two, three, and four), the analysis of the Mexican economy focuses on the structural aspects of the reform of the state regarding the external sector and the efficiency and distributional impacts of fiscal and financial reform. It goes on to show how the participation of the entire society has been increased by macroeconomic adjustment, and is now replacing the state in its role as leader of the economic development of Mexico.

Finally, in lecture three (chapter five) I summarize the way in which all these changes have brought about a profound transformation of the economy, in that it is now much better prepared to face the uncertainties of a rapidly changing and challenging world and to respond more effectively to the social needs of our population.

1

Macroeconomic Adjustment and Social Consensus: The Mexican Stabilization Program (1983–1991)

For many developing countries, the last decade has meant a protracted effort to reestablish price stability and consolidate the basis of sustained economic growth. Unfortunately, after repeated attempts at stabilization based on partial correction of budget imbalances and the balance of payments, economies often find themselves facing hyperinflation once again, weakened by capital flight and the disintegration of their financial systems and immersed in a deep recession in which standards of living are falling rapidly and unevenly.

From the point of view of the design and evaluation of economic policy, it cannot always be said that these economies are in such a disastrous state simply because their governments are not willing to follow conventional stabilization measures based on financial austerity and the realignment of the real exchange rate. In fact, the problem for the government gets worse when, in spite of all attempts to make adjustments, the results are very limited. Therefore it has become indispensable to look for non-recessive ways of controlling inflation.

Since 1985, several developing countries such as Bolivia, Israel, and Mexico have decided to move away from conventional aggregate demand adjustment programs. To stop high and persistent inflation, they have included some combination of incomes policies along with the usual fiscal and monetary measures. These stabilization programs, nonorthodox to a certain extent, represent an important change in the way in which policy makers interpret fundamental economic relationships. From this perspective, the dynamics of prices, wages, industrial structure, and the regulatory and institutional characteristics of foreign currency and financial markets help to explain both the persistent, high inflation and fiscal and monetary imbalances. The conception and implementation of programs of this type stem from the idea that monetary and public expenditure policies are not able to simultaneously achieve low inflation and avoid a deep recession. To stabilize successfully, it is also necessary to correct the inflationary momentum and structural weaknesses of economic systems.

To thoroughly explain the interaction between the institutional and macroeconomic development of the Mexican economy, this chapter has been divided into four sections. The first examines the main aspects of the inflationary and recessive crises in the developing countries. Particular emphasis is put on the influence of imperfect markets, budget rigidity, and the dynamics of price and salary contracts on the severity and duration of the crises. The next section compares the stabilization theories for developed countries, taking a nonorthodox view of structural change programs. It will also specify the scope and the limitations of monetary, fiscal, and exchange rate policies. The third section presents the background to the Pact for Economic Solidarity (Pacto de Solidaridad Económica), together with a description of the Mexican economy between 1982 and 1987. Finally, the fourth section summarizes the design and application of macroeconomic policy during the last year of President Miguel De la Madrid's government and the first three of President Salinas de Gortari. Special attention is paid to the management of monetary, fiscal, and trade policy, price and wage administration, and the role of public opinion and expectations in the consolidation of the Mexican stabilization program.

1 Inflation and Stabilization in Developing Economies: Chronology of the Typical Route to a Crisis

Developing countries' experiences with inflation are similar in many ways. An analysis of these similarities can afford us a better understanding of its dynamics and persistence. The chronology of the crises of the 1980s begins in most cases with a phase of acceleration of aggregate demand growth, almost always caused by budget overruns that upset the climate of exchange rate and prevalent price stability. At first this increase in public spending and the fiscal deficit have limited effects on internal inflation, in large part due to the fact that the rapid growth in imports in the public and private sectors is accompanied by greater foreign debt.

During this stage there is growth, an appreciation of the real exchange rate, and a substantial improvement in the standard of living; per capita consumption increases, real wages grow, and there is a reduction in the rates of unemployment and underemployment. The first negative effects of the fiscal imbalance and the foreign debt are typically felt in the financial sector. Part of the reason for this is that the change from stable growth to the acceleration phase is not backed by a corresponding flexibility in the financial system. The insufficiency of total savings and financial mediation is aggravated by the lack of an efficient money market,[1] controlled interest rates, and an excessively regulated banking system.[2] When interest rates do not reflect the magnitude of accumulated imbalances, the balance of payments begins to be dominated by capital flight.[3] As a consequence of these distortions, billions[4] of dollars in public sector and commercial bank credits are "recycled" abroad. In the meantime, the improved real exchange rate gives the public an excellent opportunity to obtain capital gains by altering the composition of their portfolios in favor of foreign currency instruments.[5]

Finally, when the current account deficit and capital flight have consumed both international reserves and new sources of transfers from abroad, the central bank withdraws from the foreign exchange market. There is a major devaluation of the real exchange rate, and it becomes necessary to seek emergency funds. In most cases, access to these funds will be conditional on the adoption of a stabilization program arranged with the International Monetary Fund (IMF). These programs usually demand substantial cuts in public spending, the realignment of relative prices (including public sector prices and tariffs), a modification of price controls in sluggish sectors , and the commitment to maintain restrictive credit policies and an undervalued real exchange rate.

The resulting recession has very unequal effects on different sectors of the population. The burden of the adjustment program tends to fall on the working classes, not only because subsidies are eliminated, but also because capital is more mobile than labor. Therefore, when foreign exchange controls do not work, it becomes even more difficult to realign the real exchange rate without lowering real wages.[6] Monetary and fiscal adjustment[7] have additional recessive effects whenever the redistributive effects of the crisis further reduce the available income in high-spending sectors. As production falls, inflation accelerates and hits the working classes once again. Even though the fiscal adjustment is consistent with the balance of payments restriction, it is insufficient because of the limited sources of non-inflationary financing and/or because of the real effect that the depreciation of the exchange rate has on the public debt. However, in many other cases stagnation, together with inflation, reflects higher input costs caused by the recessive effect of the adjusted exchange rate on aggregate supply.

When the first phase of the stabilization program has finished, the country is immersed in a deep recession, and inflation is higher and more persistent than before the crisis.[8] It would therefore seem that what is needed is an even greater recession to bring inflation back to where it was before the collapse. From an external accounts point of view, macroeconomic adjustment policies give fast results. The current account shows an important surplus due to the fall in imports, and capital repatriation is sparked by a reduction in the expected rate of depreciation.

The persistence of inflation in each case depends on structural factors.[9] The initial devaluation has a great impact on general price levels. All tradeable goods suffer price increments in their local currency in proportion to the devaluation, while the increase in the price of imported intermediate-use and capital goods affects production costs. The initial price increase is followed by an out-of-phase contractual wage raise that attempts to recover purchasing power. This increase in nominal wages will be followed by another wave of price increases. The effects of the exchange collapse set in motion a price-wage-price spiral in such a way that a "once and for all" adjustment, such as a maxi-devaluation of the exchange rate, is in fact translated into higher rates of inflation.

At the same time, the improvement in the balance of payments allows the central bank to accumulate reserves. Then it is possible to put into effect an anti-inflationary strategy based on fixing the nominal exchange rate. It is hoped that this strategy will result in a moderate, temporary appreciation in the real exchange rate. For some time the monetary authorities stop responding to nominal wage hikes with proportional increases in the nominal exchange rate, in the belief that decelerating inflation of tradeable goods and inputs will have repercussions on the prices of the other primary factors. Although inflation slows down, the momentum caused by ex post indexed contracts triggers a rise in real wages and brings about an appreciation of the real exchange rate. This stabilization strategy, known as "soft landing," usually leads to a new balance of payments crisis before inflation targets can be achieved.

In this way, only if there are adequate reserves (and/or foreign savings) or if contracts are "forward looking" can inflation "land" gradually. On the contrary, if these conditions are not satisfied, there will be a new crisis, which will require a new adjustment program based on greater fiscal and monetary austerity, adding to the frustration and incredulity of everyone involved.

2 Neoclassical Theory and Stabilization in Developing Countries

2.1 Inflation in Developed and Developing Countries

Neoclassical economic theory establishes some essential principles for the macroeconomic handling of monetary economies that are equally applicable to industrialized and developing countries. For example, there is no substitute for monetary and fiscal discipline as necessary conditions for growth with price stability. However, neoclassical macroeconomic theory, conceived in the context of institutions in developed countries, finds it difficult to explain and propose policy solutions for the inflationary processes of developing countries.

Looking at the postwar period, one may conclude that in developing countries inflation is generally higher, more volatile, and therefore more difficult to control than in industrialized nations. Although these contrasts can be partly explained by the different behavior and credibility of monetary and fiscal policies between countries, institutional aspects also come into play. In the first place, the financial structures in developing countries allowed them to depend more on the inflation tax to cover their public deficits. For example, the absence of a money market makes it more difficult to cover fiscal commitments by means of voluntary savings.[10] Regarding the volatility of inflation, because developing countries depend heavily on foreign investment and export only a limited selection of products, they are very sensitive to variations in terms of trade and interruptions in flows of funds from abroad. There are also important differences in the transmission mechanisms. In industrialized countries, an imbalance in the current account—caused either by an autonomous increase in domestic absorption or by unfavorable developments in trade agreements—results in higher interest rates to attract the flow of resources needed to fill the gap. However, where financial repression exists, interest rates do not respond. This means that if the country cannot obtain sufficient quantities of foreign investment, even with transitory fluctuations in the exogenous variables, it is forced to resort to a major devaluation and greater inflation.

The characteristics of wage contracts are also very important in explaining the persistence of inflation. Let us assume that the terms of trade have deteriorated to the point that a devaluation becomes necessary. The depreciation of the real exchange rate will last only as long as wages lag behind prices. If nominal wages rise in the same proportion as the movement in the exchange rate, another devaluation will be necessary, thereby initiating an inflation-devaluation cycle, unless the authorities prefer to induce unemployment and recession to keep the price-wage equilibrium behind the exchange rate. It is for this reason that complete and ex post indexation and the shortening of contracts can accelerate inflation from moderate levels (of the order of 40 percent per annum) to hyperinflation in a matter of months.[11]

2.2 Neoclassical Viewpoint of Stabilization (Orthodox Programs)

The neoclassical theory of economic policy, which provides the rational for the conditions imposed by the IMF[12] and for orthodox-style stabilization programs in general, places greater emphasis on the administration of aggregate demand and therefore less importance on the structural aspects of inflation. At the risk of simplification, it could be said that this viewpoint assumes that inflation is essentially a monetary phenomenon caused by the excessive expansion of credit. Therefore, it can only be corrected by restrictive monetary policy.[13] Imbalances in the balance of payments, according to this view, can only cause inflation inasmuch as surpluses are not sterilized. On the other hand, deficits will necessarily be deflationary. Monetary policy cannot, for good or for bad, have permanent effects on production and jobs. Only unanticipated changes in the money supply can affect production, meaning that any recession caused by credit policy will be transitory. As a result, costs in terms of jobs and production of any "announced" program should be low and short term, while the response from inflation and the balance of payments should be fast.[14]

The close relationship between this viewpoint and the quantitative theory of money contrasts with the less rigorous way in which changes in nominal income are divided between prices and quantities in the medium and long term. The secondary role assigned to aggregate supply factors, and its emphasis on the short term, is reflected in packages that consist almost entirely of measures that affect demand and underestimate the impact on jobs and production.

2.3 Stabilization and Structural Change

The interpretation of the economy under "nonorthodox" programs combines the principles of the neoclassical theory of aggregate demand with a more detailed study of the effect of market structure on the way in which fluctuations in nominal variables are divided between prices and quantities in the equilibrium. This viewpoint holds that inflation has an important inertial component. It can be caused by imbalances in the real sector and by maladjustments in monetary policy. Factors associated with the distribution of income, market structure, the type of wage contracts, and other institutional factors have an important role to play in explaining the behavior of aggregate demand and the inertial component of inflation. Inflation is seen as not only due to balance of payments surpluses. Adverse variations in the terms of trade may also provoke inflationary pressure through the effect of devaluation on prices and costs. The maladjustment of real wages (and other relative prices) sets off a vicious wages-prices-wages cycle.[15] Due to the persistence of inertial inflation, aggregate demand policy can have important short- and medium-term effects on real variables.

To sum up, the disappearance of the monetary and fiscal causes of inflation is not reason enough for inflation to drop. To explain this, we must analyze the two component parts of inflation: the initial surge and the propagation mechanism. The initial surge can come from expansionary monetary and fiscal policies. Once the adjustments to the exchange rate and public finances have taken place, the remaining inflation is wholly inertial. The lesson to be learned is clear. It is not enough to correct fiscal imbalances or external strangulation for stabilization to be achieved. The sources or causes of inflationary momentum must also be corrected.

3 Crisis, Fiscal Adjustment, and Hyperinflation

3.1 The Road from Stability to Inflation: A First Long-Term View of the Mexican Economy

Looking at the Mexican economy from a long-term perspective, the years of high inflation and low output growth appear to be more of an exception than the rule. For instance, between 1950 and 1970, Mexico registered a remarkable macroeconomic performance: gross domestic production expanded at an average rate of nearly 6.6 percent per year, while inflation stayed below 4.5 percent.

This era known as *desarrollo estabilizador* was in many ways the result of the ripening of those institutions brought into being by the Mexican Revolution (1910–1920), combined with a more stable performance of world markets. As will be discussed in further detail in the following chapters, the development strategy followed at that time was aimed at linking segmented markets in all parts of the country by investing heavily in infrastructure in the telecommunications, energy, and transport sectors; furthering agricultural production by means of an active land distribution policy; and industrializating through an import substitution policy which, while helping infant industries to go safely through the learning process, was expected to make them more competitive in the medium term.

During this period, these structural elements of the Mexican economic program were backed by strict fiscal and monetary discipline. Throughout these years, public sector borrowing requirements stayed consistently below 3 percent of GDP, while the available instruments of monetary control were geared toward the goal of maintaining price and exchange rate stability (see figures 1.1 and 1.2).

There is no reason to argue that, given Mexico's stage of development by the end of World War II, a strategy based on protection, financial repression, and the strong presence of the state in certain areas of production was not adequate. It is also true, however, that this set of measures should not and could not be kept in place forever. For instance, by the late 1960s it was already apparent that domestic and foreign private investment were growing more slowly than before, because protected monopolies had already achieved a strong market presence and had little incentive to keep on growing by means of higher employment and increased productivity. Therefore, a country like Mexico, pressed by

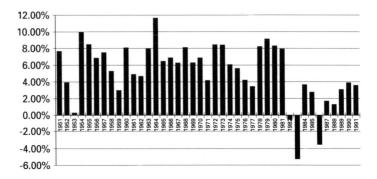

Figure 1.1
GDP annual rate of growth (1951–1991)
Source: INEGI, Cuentas Nacionales and Banco de México, Indicadores
Económicos.

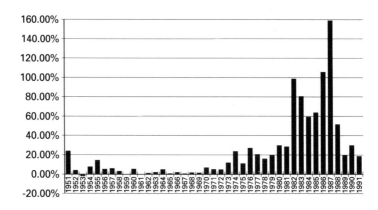

Figure 1.2
Annual rate of inflation (1951–1991)
Source: Banco de México, Indicadores Económicos.

the need to offer a workplace to a rapidly growing population, had essentially two alternatives in the 1970s: shift the aim of the development program to an export-oriented economy, as Korea had done in 1965, or continue on the path while replacing private investment with government spending. Mexico opted for the latter.

In this way, Mexico was already on the road to higher inflation as early as 1972. Between 1971 and 1976, the public sector deficit rose from slightly more than 2 percent to 9.1 percent of GDP, financed by a combination of inflation tax and external borrowing. In 1976, the country faced its first serious financial crisis since 1940 and the first devaluation of the peso against the dollar in twenty-two years.

At that time there was little question that Mexico had to undergo a profound structural transformation to restore growth and stability. However, the discovery of large oil reserves and the ability to continue borrowing in the international markets not only postponed the needed adjustment, but led the authorities to believe that the economy could grow even faster than it had in the previous two decades. For some time it was possible to grow at 8 and 9 percent per year, with inflation creeping up into the double-digit range, until the limit of external borrowing capacity was finally reached in 1982.

3.2 The First Stage of Macroeconomic Adjustment and Structural Reform: The Mexican Economy between 1982 and 1987

For Mexico, the 1982 crisis was the worst since the Great Depression. Fundamental budget and current account imbalances, combined with suspension of the inflow of foreign savings, massive deterioration of the terms of trade, and an exchange collapse, marked the beginning of a period of high inflation and economic stagnation (see table 1.1). In response to the crisis, President De la Madrid's government set in motion the Immediate Program for Economic Readjustment (PIRE by its Spanish acronym) in 1983. The idea was to correct public finances and lay the foundation for a healthier medium-term recovery. To this end, the government cut public spending substantially and increased public sector prices and tariffs. The PIRE initiatives brought about an unprecedented reduction in the primary and operational deficits. However, total financing as a share of GDP continued at a high level due to the persistence of inflation. Between 1983 and 1985, the primary balance improved by 10.7 percent of GDP, and the operational surplus by 6.3 percent. The budget, corrected for inflation, was balanced by the end of 1985 (see table 1.2).

Table 1.1
Macroeconomic indicators (1978–1991)

	Inflation	Growth of GDP
1978–81	23.6	8.4
1982	98.8	−0.6
1983	80.0	−5.2
1984	59.2	3.6
1985	63.7	2.7
1986	105.7	−3.5
1987	159.2	1.7
1988	51.6	1.3
1989	19.7	3.1
1990	29.9	4.4
1991	18.8	3.6

Source: Banco de México, Indicadores Económicos.

Table 1.2
Public finance indicators

	Public spending (% real increase)	Current/ investment spending	PSBR	Operational deficit	Primary deficit (% of GDP)
1982	−8.0	55.3	16.9	5.5	7.3
1983	−17.3	46.1	8.6	−0.4	−4.2
1984	0.8	43.2	8.5	0.3	−4.8
1985	−6.1	36.4	9.6	0.8	−3.4
1986	−13.3	34.6	15.9	2.4	−1.6
1987	−0.5	33.8	16.0	−1.8	−4.7
1988	−10.3	29.3	12.4	3.6	−8.0
1989	0.4	26.7	5.5	1.7	−7.9
1990	6.1	34.5	4.0	−2.3	−7.9
1991	3.7	37.6	1.5	−2.7	−5.6

Source: Presidency of the Republic, Criteria for Economic Policy in 1992.

The external accounts were an important constraint to economic policy making after 1982. Net transfers to Mexico plummeted. While they were 7.4 percent of GDP in 1981, they became −5.8 percent in 1985 and −5.7 percent in 1988. In this way the country moved from being a net importer of capital of the order of U.S.$12 billion per annum in 1981 to a net exporter with an outflow of more than U.S.$10 billion during the last administration.

In 1984, the government decided to reduce the rate of devaluation of the nominal exchange rate as part of the inflation control strategy. Still, inflation went down slowly. The real exchange rate appreciation started affecting manufacturing exports, particularly during the first half of 1985. Perhaps the situation was worsened by the structure of protection, which made many inputs either unavailable or very expensive. It soon became clear that a gradual stabilization package would not be able to hold up for long unless the country faced favorable conditions in the external markets. But quite the contrary happened (see table 1.3).

The September 1985 earthquakes and the drop in international oil prices in 1986 seriously affected the country's macroeconomic development. The reduction in demand for hydrocarbons and the subsequent fall in prices shrank public income by almost U.S. $9 billion that year alone—an amount equivalent to the total value of agricultural production in that year.

The supply shocks were a serious setback in the fight against inflation. Without access to world capital markets, the decline in oil prices would be translated into higher rates of inflation or a deeper recession. In that context, nonorthodox programs were being implemented in Israel, Brazil, and Argentina. However, President De la Madrid's administration avoided succumbing to the temptation of rushing into this type of program. It was better to wait until public finances were healthy and the real exchange rate and

Table 1.3
Effective real exchange rate (index, 1970 = 100.0)

1982	124.2
1983	135.2
1984	110.9
1985	106.8
1986	155.9
1987	169.4
1988	139.2
1989	128.2
1990	128.0
1991	116.4

Source: Banco de México, Indicadores Económicos.

international reserves were consistent with price stability targets (see table 1.4).

By comparing the 1986 oil crisis with the crisis of 1982, some of the more favorable consequences of the structural change programs come to light, particulary in the financial sector. This time the authorities were willing to respond to the decline in the terms of trade with higher interest rates. The effects of the liberalization of trade for intermediate goods and the correction of the real exchange rate that started in 1985 encouraged nonmanufacturing exports (see table 1.5).

A fall in real wages was the inescapable consequence of the stabilization program, but it also played an additional dual role. On the one hand, it allowed greater competitive-

Table 1.4
Balance of payments (millions U.S.$)

	Current account	Capital account	Errors and omissions	Change in reserves
1980	−10,740	11,442	98	1,018
1981	−16,052	26,357	−9,030	1,012
1982	−6,221	9,753	−6,832	−3,185
1983	5,418	−1,416	−884	3,101
1984	4,238	39	−924	3,201
1985	714	−1,809	−1,327	−2,328
1986	−1,644	1,837	410	985
1987	3,752	−576	2,924	6,924
1988	−2,521	−1,448	−2,764	−7,127
1989	−6,051	3,037	3,409	271
1990	−7,114	8,164	2,184	3,414
1991	−13,283	20,179	1,241	7,821

Source: Banco de México, Indicadores Económicos.

Table 1.5
Trade balance ($U.S. millions)

	Oil exports	Non-oil exports	Private imports	Public imports
1982	16,477	4,752	9,036	5,400
1983	16,017	6,295	4,244	4,306
1984	16,601	7,594	6,464	4,789
1985	14,776	6,897	8,825	4,386
1986	6,307	9,723	8,089	3,343
1987	8,629	12,026	10,524	2,780
1988	6,709	13,835	16,721	3,552
1989	7,876	14,966	21,667	3,771
1990	10,104	16,735	27,025	4,246
1991	8,166	18,954	35,331	2,853

Source: Banco de México, Indicadores Económicos.

ness of exports from labor-intensive sectors and promoted in-bond industries. At the same time it consolidated the contraction in demand. Between 1982 and 1987, the general minimum wage suffered a reduction of 44.6 percent in real terms, while contractual wages, including benefits, dropped by 40.5 percent. In spite of the magnitude of the crisis, it was possible to avoid massive company shutdowns and the uncontrollable growth of unemployment. In fact, permanent employment grew, according to information furnished by the IMSS (Mexican Social Security Institute), at an average annual rate of 3.5 percent during the same period—slightly higher than the growth of the work force (see table 1.6).

A serious financial crisis interrupted the economic recovery with the collapse of the Mexican Stock Market by the end of 1987. In part it was caused by the fall of the New

Table 1.6
Index of employment and real wages (1982 = 100.0)

	Workers inscribed permanently in the Social Security Institute	Growth (%)	Minimum wage in real terms[1]	Contractual wage in real terms[2]
1982	100.0	−1.7	100.0	100.0
1983	99.6	−0.3	71.3	68.5
1984	107.3	7.7	67.3	63.5
1985	114.9	7.0	66.0	66.9
1986	112.2	−2.3	59.0	61.1
1987	122.9	9.5	55.4	59.5
1988	129.8	5.6	48.3	47.6
1989	131.3	1.2	50.8	45.6
1990	141.0	7.4	46.2	42.2
1991	148.6	5.4	46.0[3]	47.5

Source: IMSS.
1. Source: National Commission for the Minimum Wage (end of the period).
2. Source: Presidential state of the nation address, annex. Datum for 1991 to June.
3. November 1991 versus November 1990.

York Stock Exchange and the other major international financial centers, and in part it resulted from administrative errors. The mood of uncertainty caused by this collapse and a monthly inflationary momentum of 6 percent resulted in intense capital flight that culminated in the November 1987 devaluation, setting the country off toward hyperinflation. Faced with this situation, the Mexican government had to decide whether to embark upon another attempt at orthodox stabilization or to combine fiscal adjustment with powerful measures to achieve structural change and combat inflationary momentum.

Choosing the first option would very probably have meant a further drop in the general standard of living, while the second, with the lower public expectations, meant the possibility of meeting the same fate as other income policy programs, which had failed a short time before.

3.3 Designing a Stabilization Program for Mexico

During the first five years of President De la Madrid's administration, an enormous fiscal adjustment effort was made with the understanding that it was a prerequisite for successful stabilization. It was well known that before embarking on a strategy based on nominal price anchors, it was indispensable to have sufficient international reserves, a current account surplus, and a significant public finance primary surplus. In addition to the purely technical difficulties presented by the design of a strategy consistent with macroeconomic targets, the administration faced the serious problem of implementing new initiatives in its last year of government. The credibility of the program was at risk. Furthermore, the world was facing a financial crisis, and Mexico had problems in the foreign exchange market caused by disorder in the stock market. It was precisely to take the expectation problem by the horns, thereby avoiding the uncontrollable flight of capital, that the need to reconcile recession with hyperinflation was recognized.

Moreover, it should be mentioned that as the Mexican government was evaluating the implementation of measures like the Pact for Economic Solidarity, the austral and cruzado programs were collapsing deafeningly. This would make it even more difficult to maintain an atmosphere of tranquillity in the various sectors and muster their support. The government had followed closely the evolution of the Argentine and Brazilian economies, however, trying to learn from their mistakes and ensure that the same thing would not happen in Mexico.

3.3.1 Why Do Stabilization Programs Fail?

When the characteristics of the Pact had to be defined, it was still not possible to be sure of the effectiveness of so-called nonorthodox programs. They had yielded catastrophic results in Brazil and Argentina and acceptable results in Israel and Bolivia. After an analysis of these cases, the conclusion was drawn that the most common faults were related to at least one of the following factors:

Incomplete fiscal reform. A small operational deficit is a necessary condition for successful stabilization—more so if financial markets have been destroyed or weakened. It is not possible to stabilize if the inflation tax is still needed to bridge the fiscal gap, which was what happened in the case of Brazil and Argentina.[16]

Incomplete change in the institutions that create price momentum. Destroying momentum requires a change in price formation mechanisms. This includes the elimination of wage indexation and the liberalization of trade. For example, quarterly wage revisions were reinstated, and a stepped-up exchange rate and official price increases started again after the first stage of the austral plan in Argentina. The result was a return to inertial inflation and accommodative monetary policy. Liberalization of trade, in addition to having a favorable impact on productive efficiency in the medium and long terms, permits short-term stabilization of the prices of tradeables. In neither Brazil nor Argentina were trade barriers reduced to bring about an effective control over the price of tradeables and thus nontradeables.[17]

Excessive expansion of aggregate demand above the bearable limits set by the restriction of foreign savings. The elimination of the inflation tax is reflected in a rapid aggregate demand growth and current account deterioration. This happened in Brazil, Argentina, and Israel. The difference in Israel's case is that expansion was compensated for by increases in transfers from abroad.

Inadequate relative prices. Wherever there are price controls, some sectors lag considerably behind others for the duration of the program. If there is no consensus-gathering mechanism to take care of these stragglers without inflation (for example, increasing some prices and lowering others), the consensus on the program's effectiveness will be weakened, which can bring about its failure.[18]

Taking these factors into account, the new stabilization strategy based on consensus gathering, fiscal adjustment, and determination to solve the problem of transfers abroad was designed.

4 The Pact for Economic Solidarity and the Pact for Stability and Economic Growth[19]

4.1 Conception and Design of the Pact: Chronology

On 15 December 1987, the president of the republic and representatives of the labor, farming, and business sectors signed the Pact. From then on, the government of Mexico worked arduously to guarantee the program's success. For example, in the months that followed the Pact's signing, the economic cabinet met three times a week in the presence of the president. Furthermore, between December 1987 and November 1988 the Follow-up Commission held thirty-two ordinary and four extraordinary meetings to monitor the carrying out of commitments outlined in the agreement. This was how Mexico, with the participation of all sectors, achieved important advances in structural change and the control of inflation.

The Pact was designed with the following objectives in mind:

• Continuing commitment to the permanent correction of public finance. Structural change received special emphasis, with the enactment of measures designed to reduce the size of the public administration and privatize state-run companies.

• Restrictive monetary policy. Credit expansion, once inflation and foreign reserve targets had been set, only took place as expectations and growth reactivation consolidated.

• Correction of wage momentum. Agreements with the workers focused on moving away from short-term contracts with complete ex post indexation toward longer contracts defined in terms of anticipated inflation (ex ante indexation).

• Agreement on prices in leader sectors. A pragmatic policy of price coordination cannot include all goods in the economy: deflation will result from the fixing of primary input prices and prices in leader sectors. Internal competition and control of aggregate demand helps to reduce inflation in nontradeables.

• Liberalization of trade. The "law of one price" should begin to work (albeit slowly) to place an upper boundary on the prices of tradeables and help knock down the cost of intermediate goods.

• Control of inflation and the negotiation of leader prices instead of total price freezing. Instead of establishing immediate targets of zero inflation, positive and diminishing inflation targets are set, with the aim of avoiding too rapid an expansion in aggregate demand in relation to the production of goods.

• Adoption of measures based on negotiated price controls. Any program of controls must be perceived as sustainable in the medium term, to avoid speculation and hoarding. For this to happen, the consensus of all participating sectors is indispensable.

The goverment therefore entered consensus gathering with a commitment to respect a real, permanent, and visible fiscal adjustment. It was not only reflected in a reduction of ordinary spending, but in a solid program of privatization and the shutdown of state-run companies that were costing the state too much. The private sector had to commit itself to sacrificing its profit margins, while the labor and agricultural sectors sacrificed an increase in real wages.

As of phase two of the PSE, as expectations of the program's success were raised, it was possible to guarantee the stability of public prices, wages, and the exchange rate for longer and longer periods of time. At the same time, advances continued to be made in the structural change of public finances and foreign trade

The Pact has gone through ten stages, whose different characteristics are described in table 1.7. The first of these combined fiscal adjustment, realignment of relative prices, and protection of the purchasing power of wages with a monetary and exchange policy aimed at containing the growth of the general price level.

Table 1.7
The Pact (chronology)

Pact for Economic Solidarity	Pact for Stability and Economic Growth
Phase 1 (December 1987– February 1988) • Tax measures: elimination of subsidies except to agriculture. Elimination of the accelerated depreciation incentive and an additional import tax (5%). • Public price and free adjustments. • Reduction in programmable spending by 1.5% of GDP. • Exchange rate policy to support deflation without sacrificing competitiveness. • Trade policy: reduction of the maximum import tariff from 40% to 20%, and elimination of permits. • Immediate minimum wage rise of 15%; 20% rise in January. Monthly review according to anticipated inflation (ex ante). • Guaranteed prices for agricultural products to be kept at their real levels of 1987. • Price agreements for basic products.	*Phase 1 (January 1989–July 1989)* • Fiscal budget consistent with lower inflation and gradual economic recovery. • Public sector prices with greater incidence over CPI will remain constant. Some prices to commerce and industry rise, but entrepreneurs agree on absorbing the impact. • The exchange rate of the peso against the dollar was to crawl 1 peso a day. • Reduction of the import tariff spread. • It is agreed that controlled prices will be revised on a case-by-case basis. • Support prices for agricultural products will be revised to maintain their real levels. Price of fertilizers remains constant.
Phase 2 (March 1988) • Constant public sector goods prices and tariffs. • Exchange rate fixed at the level of 2/29/1988. • No price tariff or controlled price rise. • 3% rise in the minimum and contractual wages. • Corresponding adjustment to guaranteed prices. • Through consensus gathering, pact to freeze leader prices.	*Phase 2 (August 1989–March 1990)* • Public sector prices to remain constant. • The crawling peg remains at 1 peso at day. • Firms agree to maintain their price levels and to guarantee supply. • Controlled prices are reviewed on a case-by-case basis. • The government stresses its commitment to speeding up the regulation process.

Table 1.7 (continued)

Pact for Economic Solidarity	Pact for Stability and Economic Growth
Phase 3 (April 1988–May 1988) • Fixed public sector prices and fees. • Fixed exchange rate until May 31. • No increase in registered or controlled prices. • Fixed minimum wage. • Businesspeople make a commitment to defend the purchasing power of the minimum wage.	*Phase 3 (January 1990–December 1990)* • Revision to minimum wages to keep purchasing power in line with expected inflation. • Crawling peg set at 80 centavos a day. • Adjustment to public sector prices to comply with the revenue goals in the budget. • Revision of controlled prices on a case-by-case basis.
Phase 4 (June 1988–August 1988) • Fixed public sector prices and fees. • Fixed exchange rate until August 31. • Prices subject to registration and control are fixed. • Fixed minimum wage.	*Phase 4 (December 1990–December 1991)* • Revision of minimum wages to keep purchasing power. • Crawl of the peso vs. the dollar down to 40 centavos a day. • Public sector prices are increased in November 1990 to meet the primary surplus goals for 1991, but they will remain constant throughout 1991. • Workers and employers sign a National Productivity Program. • Case-by-case revision of controlled prices.
Phase 5 (September 1988–December 1988) • Constant prices and fees. • Fixed exchange rate. • Value-added tax reduction from 6% to 0% in unprocessed foods and medicines. • Income tax reduction of 30% for people who earn up to four times the minimum wage. • Minimum wage remains fixed. • Businesspeople sign an agreement to lower prices by 3% (prices effectively dropped by 2.87%).	*Phase 5 (December 1991–December 1992)* • Revision of minimum wages to keep purchasing power. • The crawl of the peso vs. the dollar is slowed to 20 centavos a day. The dual exchange rate regime is eliminated. • Public sector prices are adjusted to meet the budget goal. • Value-added tax is reduced from 15% to 10%. • Prices to be revised on a case-by-case basis.

The following section presents a description of each of these criteria and the ways in which they are reflected in monetary, fiscal, trade, and price policy and the impact they have had on inflation, economic activity, jobs, and expectations.

4.2 Economic Policy during the Pact

For the last four years, the macroeconomic adjustment effort has been accompanied by a wide range of structural reforms, including fiscal reform, privatization of state-owned enterprises, renegotiation of the external debt, financial reform, and trade liberalization—all of them part of a single integral program. Although in the next chapters there will be an opportunity to comment in more detail on the long-term effects of each of these reforms, the following paragraphs emphasize the point of contact between macro and micro policies in the context of a stabilization program.

4.2.1 Public Finance Policy

To guarantee the success of the stabilization program, it was indispensable to consolidate the fiscal achievements of the previous five years. To that end, fiscal policy has focused on three main areas. First, central government spending has been kept under tight control. Bureaucratic expenditures have been cut and reoriented toward the most pressing social needs. Second, on the side of income policy, there has been in-depth fiscal reform and a realignment of public prices and fees to international and free-market levels. Finally, the public sector has undergone a process of restructuring through the divestiture of non-strategic state-run enterprises.

Fiscal aggregates.[20]   Between 1988 and 1991, the primary surplus of the public sector reached an average level of 7 percent of GDP, the highest ever recorded in Mexican economic history. During the first year of the Pact, programmable spending underwent a reduction of 8.9 percent, in real terms, as a result of measures applied to most of the government's activities. These gains in fiscal correction were carefully respected in the following years. For example, during 1989 and 1990 current spending of the federal government and the parastatal sector was kept at the average rate of growth of the overall economy.

To carry out an adjustment of this magnitude on a permanent basis, an austerity agreement was signed (*Official Gazette*, 4 January 1988). It included, among other measures, staff reductions of 13,000 executive positions and a more efficient use of material resources. A voluntary retirement program was also put into effect to reduce the public work force by another 50,000. Additionally, a selective cancellation of programs and projects was enacted. Even though the budget adjustment meant a sizeable reduction of programmable spending in the federal public sector, it did not affect social spending. Programmable spending on social development, education, health, regional and urban development, and the National Solidarity Program against Poverty has logged a 40 percent growth in real terms during the first half of President Salinas's administration (see figure 1.3).

To reinforce the reduction initiatives aimed at public spending, special attention was paid to the calendar of disbursements. In this way, nonpriority disbursements authorized by Congress were postponed for as long as possible. Accumulated inflation for the year reduced the

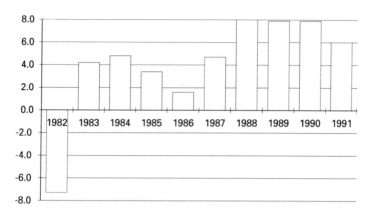

Figure 1.3
Primary surplus (% of GDP)
Source: Criteria for Economic Policy in 1992, Presidency of the Republic.

real impact of public sector disbursements. Table 1.8 shows how the largest part of the year's primary surplus was obtained during the first semesters, while the last quarters registered surpluses that averaged 13.8 percent of the yearly efforts between 1988 and 1991. This schedule resulted from the deferment of the expense and the inevitable, predictable reduction in real income due to the slow growth of public sector prices and fees.

Together with the initiatives to cut public spending, the level of subsidies and transfers was reduced. The elimination of price differentials for energy and basic petrochemical products and the reduction of financial transfers to development banks were among the most important actions in this area.

Revenue policy. The implementation of the initiatives introduced in the fiscal reform of 1989–1991, together with public sector price and fee adjustments from the very start of the

Table 1.8
Calendar of public finances[1]

		Primary surplus (%)
1988	I	41.8
	II	77.9
	III	97.4
	IV	100.0
1989	I	20.3
	II	49.6
	III	86.8
	IV	100.0
1990	I	29.8
	II	58.8
	III	83.5
	IV	100.0
1991	I	26.9
	II	55.3
	III	77.0
	IV	100.0

Source: DGPH, Ministry of Finance. The table refers to the percentage of the total yearly surplus accumulated at the end of the quarter.
1. The real collection loss suffered by the government in times of high inflation due to the time taken to collect, between the moment at which they are accrued and the time they are actually received.

stabilization program and the gradual disappearance of the Tanzi effect,[21] represented additional public revenues of around 2.2 percent of GDP per year since 1988. Moreover, the 1989–1991 tax reform made it possible to lower rates while increasing overall tax collection through broader tax bases for both corporations and individuals. Between 1989 and the present, the maximum individual income tax rate has gone down from 50 percent to 35 percent, and the corporate tax rate has decreased from 42 percent to 35 percent. Tax loopholes and special status categories have been drastically reduced and the tax administration has waged an all-out campaign against tax evasion. These measures have helped make the tax burden more equitable, while increasing credibility in the program.

The global impact of income and spending initiatives is summarized in table 1.9. What is outstanding is the primary surplus increase of almost 3.3 points of GDP during the first year of the Pact, and the drop in the public sector financial deficit by almost 15 points of GDP between 1987 and 1991.

Structural change.   The privatization of public companies is worthy of comment. Over the last three years the processes of sale, liquidation, merger, or closing have been carried out for 310 state-run organizations in the fishing, sugar, energy, telecommunications, banking, and mining sectors. As a result, more than 80 percent of the 1,115 state-run companies that existed in 1982 were no longer in the hands of the government by the end of 1991. During this administration, there has been a particularly significant advance in the divestiture of public enterprises such as the two major national airlines (Mexicana and Aeroméxico), one of the world's largest copper mines (Compañía Minera de Cana-

Table 1.9
Public finance indicators (% of GDP)

	1987	1988	1989	1990	1991
Total revenues	28.4	28.1	27.2	27.5	26.2
PEMEX	11.7	9.9	8.9	9.0	8.0
Federal government	9.5	10.9	12.2	12.2	12.3
Taxes	8.6	9.3	10.1	10.6	10.8
Nontaxes	0.9	1.6	2.1	1.6	1.5
Total expenditures	43.8	40.5	34.4	30.6	26.7
Nonprogrammable expenditures	23.5	21.4	16.9	13.3	9.2
Domestic interest payments	15.7	13.7	9.8	7.5	3.5
Foreign interest payments	4.5	3.9	3.6	2.6	2.2
Programmable expenditures	20.3	19.1	17.5	17.3	17.5
Current expenditures	12.3	11.9	11.1	11.2	10.9
Capital expenditures	4.5	3.7	3.2	3.8	3.4
Deficit of financial mediation	1.0	1.6	0.6	1.1	1.0
PSBR	16.0	12.4	5.5	4.0	1.5
Operational deficit	−1.8	3.6	1.7	−2.3	−2.7
Primary deficit	−4.7	−8.0	−7.9	−7.9	−5.6

Source: DPGH-DGPI, Ministry of Finance. The numbers for 1991 are taken from Criterios, Presidency of the Republic.
Note: The upper numbers exclude the noncontrolled parastatal sector. Programmable spending includes expenditures, capital expenditures, and transfers to noncontrolled enterprises.

nea), the national telephone company (Telmex), and the commercial banks. The divestiture process not only has a one-time impact through the revenues from the sale of parastatal firms, but also a permanent reduction in transfers to firms that were not viable and were shut down. For instance, since the beginning of the Pact, total revenues from sales are around $14.5 billion, which have been used in large part to reduce the stock of internal debt. Overall transfers from the federal government have gone down from almost 6 percent of GDP in 1987 to around 2 percent in 1991. An important feature of the fiscal effect of privatization is that it is permanent. Government outlays for the operation of these firms are cut once and for all, whereas emergency budget cuts in other areas, such as investments, can not be sustained indefinitely.

4.2.2 The Renegotiation of the External Debt

When the goal is to stabilize only through aggregate demand instruments, what usually happens is that, in spite of an improvement in public finances corrected for inflation and the balance of payments, inflation—due almost strictly to inertia—stays high. For example, although the primary surplus increased by more than 10 GDP points between 1982 and 1985, inflation only came down from 98 percent to 64 percent per annum. Per capita GDP fell at an average yearly rate of 2.5 percent.

When the inertial component has been eliminated, observed inflation ("minimum sustainable inflation") depends on which of the restrictions—the balance of payments (maximum deficit in current account given the availability of external savings) or public finances (constant relationship of debt with GDP)—becomes relevant first. In most cases, the levels of forced savings required to satisfy the foreign restriction imply higher inflation than that required to cover a moderate operational deficit. From this level, any drop in inflation due to a reduction in domestic public spending does not mean that there is less need for an inflation tax consistent with the public borrowing capacity. On the contrary, inflation is such that forced saving induces the involuntary withdrawal of total public debt. In reality, the lowest level of inflation corresponds to the fall in forced savings needed to satisfy the levels of transfers abroad implicit in the service of the foreign debt.

The most effective way to reduce inflation in these cases is by lowering the net transfer of resources abroad. When the balance of payments is the most relevant restriction, additional cuts in the domestic budget have a very reduced impact on inflation. The relaxing of the foreign restriction enhances progress in both inflation and growth. This means that upon the conclusion of the internal correction of 1988, the next step in the stabilization process and transition toward growth necessarily had to come from renegotiation of the foreign debt, as in fact happened during the first year of President Salinas de Gortari's term. Table 1.10 shows the cost of the public sector's foreign debt. This information underscores the fact that servicing the foreign debt cost almost 8 percent of GDP during the years of adjustment, which implies levels of net transfers abroad of nearly 7 percent of GDP.

It should be pointed out that the Pact was set in motion without the help of the International Monetary Fund. The foreign creditors were not willing to recognize that Mexico's program was based on the enormous efforts of the previous years, and that adequate internal macroeconomic preconditions existed. Commercial banks and multilateral credi-

Table 1.10
Indicators of the cost of Mexico's foreign debt (% of GDP)

	Net transfers	Debt service
1982	5.4	10.1
1983	7.6	12.9
1984	6.1	8.8
1985	5.8	8.5
1986	2.9	8.9
1987	1.6	8.3
1988	5.7	7.0
1989	−0.3	6.4
1990	−2.6	5.2
1991	−5.8	5.2

Source: SAFI, Ministry of Finance.

tors refused to open negotiations with the De la Madrid government, preferring to wait for the new administration. During the first months of President Salinas de Gortari's administration, the negotiations with commercial banks, the Paris Club, the IMF, and the World Bank finally allowed Mexico and the creditors to agree on a financing package that included an exchange operation to reduce the balance of outstanding foreign debt in an amount equivalent to the discounts reflected in the secondary market of the Mexican debt, given the resources available for the operation. As a result, the level of net transfers fell to around 3 percent of GDP. With this and the other structural change measures, Mexico has not only renewed access to international credit on a voluntary basis, but the repatriation of capital and new foreign direct investment have allowed the economy to return to a negative level of net transfers, which is normal for a labor-abundant, capital-scarce country.

4.2.3 Monetary Policy during the Pact

The monetary policy adopted during the process of stabilization had two elements. First, the Banco de México prevented abrupt movements of the rate of exchange through a very restrictive credit policy. The authorities have speeded up the process of financial innovation and reform to facilitate the capital repatriation and further financial intermediation needed to allow the economy to respond to emerging investment opportunities.

During the first months of the Pact, the role of the central bank was particularly important in designing an adequate credit policy for the difficult transition from hyperinflation to moderate inflation. At that time, real interest rates skyrocketed, but it was difficult to discern the true cause of the increase. It could have been caused by two entirely different circumstances, each of which implied an opposite monetary response.

Perhaps interest rates had gone up simply because the fall in expected inflation, and the subsequent reduction in the inflation tax, had stimulated an increase in the demand for peso-denominated balances. If the money supply remains constant, the result is a substantial rise in interest rates to clear the credit market. Under these circumstances, high real rates reflect an excess demand for money, and therefore the right monetary policy is to monetize. This is not a new method of stopping hyperinflation; in fact, in several other cases it was prescribed that at the moment when inflation stops via price controls, an increase in the stock of money on a once-and-for-all basis should take place in order to avoid the contractionary effects of the rise in money demand.

The second alternative is that rates might be high because they reflected an exchange risk premium that had to be paid due to the enormous uncertainty of an economy in transition. In this case, the worst policy would be to increase the monetary aggregates. Given the degree of international capital mobility in Mexico, such an action would have translated directly into capital flight and a devaluation that would have marked an end to the whole stabilization strategy.[22]

The challenge of monetary policy was therefore to find a rule that would simultaneously prevent credit strangulation and an exchange rate collapse. The shortening of public debt maturities during the first weeks (and in the weeks preceding the ratification of the Pact) was a sure sign that the reason for the high rates was linked more to uncertainty than to an increase in the demand for money.[23] This compelled the monetary authorities to wait and set up an implicit rule to systematically reduce flows of credit to the government, and only partially sterilize capital inflows, so that the expansion of credit could support the reactivation of the economy.

This environment of uncertainty has gradually given way to longer debt maturities and lower interest rates pushed by the repatriation of flown capital and further financial mediation and not by an expansionary monetary policy carried out by the Banco de México (see figures 1.4 and 1.5 and table 1.11). Parallel to the short-term credit policy, the authorities implemented a series of measures to strengthen the role of private financial savings in supporting new investment. For this reason, there has been an intense process of reform in three areas. First, new financial instruments with longer maturities and flexible rates were created to offer a better way to make intertemporal and intergenerational transfers among economic agents, while hedging against inflation and exchange rate risk. The second area of

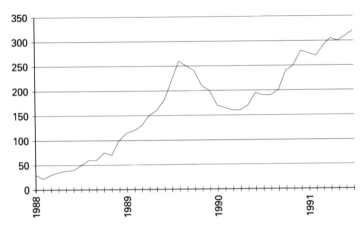

Figure 1.4
Average maturity of government debt (days)
Source: DGPH, Ministry of Finance.

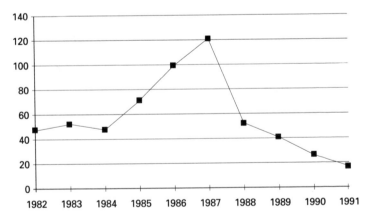

Figure 1.5
28-day Treasury bill rates (percent per annum)
Source: DGPH, Ministry of Finance.

Table 1.11
Monetary variables

		Real rates of growth		Real interest rate (28-day CETES)
		M1	M4	
1988	I	−12.4	−23.1	4.92
	II	16.6	−14.7	11.37
	III	21.2	−13.4	19.38
	IV	4.3	0.4	29.11
1989	I	9.6	14.7	7.48
	II	1.7	19.4	17.44
	III	7.1	26.2	25.46
	IV	17.0	25.7	29.77
1990	I	14.0	19.5	2.16
	II	19.1	17.3	6.30
	III	13.1	14.8	9.06
	IV	27.1	12.1	8.48
1991	I	10.5	16.2	0.14
	II	11.1	16.3	2.04
	III	10.5	13.9	3.87
	IV	10.8	9.4	1.90

Source: Elaborated with information from the Banco de México. The real rates of CETES correspond to the anualized yield of a peso invested in CETES on the first day of the year and continuously reinvested.

reform included establishing a regulatory framework to modernize financial intermediaries. In December 1989, Congress approved a legislative package that included measures to strengthen the presence of brokerage houses and the stock exchange, insurance companies, leasing companies and warehouses, as well as the development of financial groups. The third element has been the reprivatization of commercial banks.

In practice, financial reform has been essential for backing the prudent credit policy of the Banco de México so that an unbearable cost in terms of activity and employment could be avoided. Therefore, the combination of fiscal adjustment and the development of a credit market to handle the financing of public sector borrowing requirements has translated into a substantial reduction in the reliance on central bank funds for financing the federal government, which in turn represents lower inflationary pressure. The bottom line is that during 1990 the total amount of credit received by the nonfinancial government sector from the central bank declined by 11.3 percent in real terms. During 1991 the government was able to reduce its debt balance with the Banco de México by another 35 percent in real terms (see table 1.12).

4.2.4 Negotiated Price Control Policy

Probably one of the most controversial aspects of non-orthodox stabilization programs deals with price controls. It is undeniable that where there is inertial inflation, it is difficult to bring about stabilization through aggregate demand policies alone. If more importance were placed on minimum inflation consistent with fiscal restrictions and the balance of payments than on implicit control targets, however, the result would be shortages, black markets, and the eventual failure of the program.

Table 1.12
Percentage changes on the balance of financing of the Banco de México to the nonfinancial public sector (real term)

1981	11.1
1982	27.8
1983	−12.6
1984	−18.2
1985	−10.6
1986	−11.6
1987	−45.4
1988	−2.2
1989[1]	40.1
1990	−11.3
1991	−35.2

1. Includes the credits for guarantees in the exchange operation of UMS for Brady bonds. Without this operation, the real increase for the year would have been 25%.

Price and wage administration under the Pact used strict criteria to help achieve aggregate targets without creating greater microeconomic distortions.[24] The Pact was based on agreements from sector to sector, which meant that special cases received special treatment to achieve global inflation targets. Price negotiation was particularly focused on leader sectors, to take advantage of oligopolistic market structures inherited from the protectionism of previous decades. In the first stage, a hefty initial public sector price and fee adjustment was made to correct lags. These were later stabilized, thereby reducing cost pressures on inflation. The support of trade associations was sought. For example, the National Association of Self-service and Discount Shops (ANTAD) played a useful role as effective price watchdogs.

Not only was the price behavior of tradeables considered, but attention was also paid to links in the production chain. Thus the costs were distributed fairly between final producers, input producers, and consumers. The prices of tradeables, in view of the recent liberalization of trade, were automatically determined by foreign prices and exchange rate policy. Trade liberalization plays a crucial role in the stabilization of the prices of more than 50 percent of the country's total production. Fixing the exchange rate against the dollar during the first year, and later on the predetermined crawling peg, was a major factor in the diminishing of inflationary pressure. More than on freezing prices, the Pact focused on controlling inflation. A target of zero inflation from the outset, apart from provoking a serious recession, would have proved too sensitive to variations in the terms of trade.

The objective of the Pact was to reduce inertial inflation, as opposed to forcing inflation down. That was why fiscal discipline and prudent price controls were indispensable. Figure 1.6 shows a comparison of the shortage indexes of the Pact with the austral and cruzado plans. In Mexico the shortage index has never been above 10 percent, whereas in Argentina and Brazil it passed the 20 percent and 40 percent mark, respectively, during the first twelve months.

In addition to macroeconomic considerations, the controls and bargaining mechanisms have had positive microeconomic results. It has come to light that price control in sectors of greatest industrial concentration result in lower shortage indexes, which is perfectly consistent with the basic principles of industrial organization theory. (See figure 1.6.)[25] Another interesting fact is that in economies in disinflation, the role of the government is crucial, to eliminate not only wage inertia but also other kinds of inertia that have to do with competition among producers and market structure. One example of this was given during

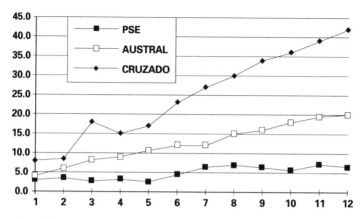

Figure 1.6
Shortage index (months after the implementation of program)
Source: Banco de México, and the central banks of Argentina and Brazil.

the third round of the PSE negotiations. At that time, businesspeople felt that given the trend of the economy, the price level of some products was simply too high for the market to bear; however, if one of the suppliers were to lower its price unilaterally, there was the possibility of a price war that would make things worse for all producers. This bleak scenario prevented them from making an initial price reduction, unless it could be accomplished in a coordinated manner. In the context of the Commission of the Pact, in the presence of the authorities, businesspeople agreed on a general uncontrolled price reduction of 3 percent.[26]

4.2.5 Trade and Exchange Rate Policies
Budget discipline and the liberalization of trade, along with the negotiation mechanism, were the Pact's most important structural measures. Negotiation with the producers of nontradeables and the lowering of trade barriers in the

tradeables sectors were indispensable for breaking down inertia. Consensus and a tendency toward purchasing power parity could reinforce each other to bring down inflation. Table 1.13 shows how the dynamics of trade liberalization coincide with the advent of the Pact, starting with the elimination of non-tariff barriers and continuing with the reduction in import duties. At present, only 9.1 percent of the production of tradeables require a permit, with an average tariff of 13.1 percent and a maximum of 20 percent.

Figure 1.7 shows the shares of tradeables and nontradeables in the consumer price index. It is clear that the price levels of tradeables have followed the behavior of the nominal exchange rate very closely, which is not the case when economies are closed and very distorted. This confirms the valuable microeconomic impact that trade opening has had—not to mention its role in terms of efficiency. Further discussion of this issue will follow in a subsequent chapter.

The trade balance and the current account have moved from a surplus before the Pact to a sizeable deficit at present. However, in contrast with what happened in the years

Table 1.13
Dynamics of trade liberalization (percentages)

	Average tariff	Import permit coverage[1]
1983	27.0	100.0
1985	22.6	35.1
1988	13.1	21.2
1989	12.1	18.4
1990	10.4	13.7
1991	13.1	9.1

Source: SECOFI.
1. Percentage of total value of imports subject to permits.

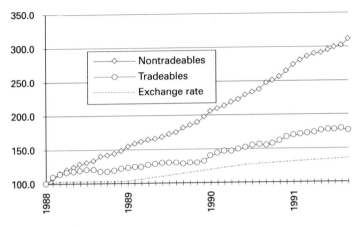

Figure 1.7
Price level of tradeable and nontradeable goods
Source: Prepared with information of Banco de México's Indicadores
Económicos.

before the crisis, this is not a reflection of an overheated
economy driven by government spending and external
overborrowing, but of a rapid expansion of investment
automatically financed with capital repatriation, direct
flows from foreign companies, and voluntary international
lending to the private sector. Consequently, in spite of the
size of the deficit, it has been possible to accumulate
reserves that in November 1991 were around U.S. $16 bil-
lion, the highest figure ever recorded for Mexico (see table
1.14).

The figures confirm the notion that the deterioration of
the trade balance is linked to a much healthier recovery.
The bulk of imports falls in the capital and intermediate
goods categories of the private sector, which will eventually
become exports or import substitutes. It is also worth mentioning that many of these imports are the counterpart of

Table 1.14
Trade balance (% variations with respect to previous year)

	1987	1988	1989	1990	1991
Total exports	27.8	0.3	11.2	17.5	1.0
Fishing and agriculture	−26.5	8.2	5.0	23.3	9.7
Mining	13.0	14.6	−8.4	2.0	−11.4
Manufacturing	40.0	18.0	9.6	10.7	14.9
Oil and natural gas	36.8	−22.2	17.3	28.3	−19.2
Total imports	7.0	52.4	25.5	22.9	22.1
Intermediate	14.9	44.6	19.1	12.9	24.2
Consumer goods	−9.3	150.3	82.1	45.7	10.6
Capital formation	−11.0	53.1	18.4	42.4	24.8

Source: Banco de México, Indicadores Económicos.

an unprecedented increase in foreign investment arising from the increase in confidence in the country and the possibility of having a North American free trade area. In many cases these imports have the additional advantage of representing a much needed technological transfer.

Finally, fiscal and trade reforms affect the trade statistics. In the case of consumer goods, it is undeniable that registered imports have grown, which does not mean that total consumer imports have grown in the same proportion. According to the new trade rules, goods that were previously smuggled are now registered, which results in a transfer from the errors and omissions account to the current account in the balance of payments.

4.3 Inflation, Employment, and Output during the Pact

The economic strategy based on fiscal and monetary discipline, consensus gathering, and the reform of the state has already yielded very encouraging results, not only in terms of short-term macroeconomic performance, but also in creating new prospects for sounder long-term growth. The scenario of serious instability has been replaced by one in which inflation is in the range of 20 percent per year and falling rapidly, and output expands at twice the pace of population. On the institutional side, the mechanism of communication within the Pact has become a unique forum for participation in the modernization of the country. Finally, as the macroeconomic environment gets more predictable and public confidence in the authorities grows, there is a greater opportunity to speed up structural change in areas such as trade, deregulation, financial liberalization, privatization, agriculture, and the fight against poverty.

It is very difficult to get a full sense of the extent of the change undergone by Mexico by simply looking at a few macroeconomic indicators. More concretely, between 1987 and 1991, December–December inflation of the consumer price index dropped from 159.2 percent to 18.5 percent. This reduction becomes even more impressive if we look at the performance of monthly inflation, which in the first month of 1988 reached an annual rate of nearly 600 percent (see figures 1.8 and 1.9).

This good inflation performance is underlined by the fact that, in spite of the very large size of the aggregate demand adjustment, the economy not only avoided going into a major recession and unemployment, but growth resumed gradually and strongly. In 1988, real GDP grew 1.3 percent; in 1989, 3.1 percent; in 1990, 4.4 percent; and it is expected that this figure for 1991 will also be around 3.6 percent (see figure 1.10).

Looking at the sources of growth on the demand side, the reactivation of private consumption spending can pri-

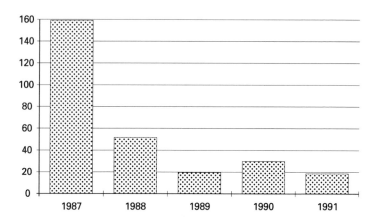

Figure 1.8
Inflation
Source: Banco de México, Indicadores Económicos.

marily be put down to the stabilization of real wages, the reduction of the inflation tax, the behavior of real interest rates, and trade and exchange policy. The first three factors refer to the effect the Pact had, and still has, on the available family income. Wage earners and other low-income groups, who usually pay the inflation tax, have benefited directly from falling inflation and the stabilization of the purchasing power of their gross income. Savers also see their available income grow due to higher real interest rates. As long as the trade liberalization and exchange rate policies are thought to be permanent, total import expenditure will increase overall microeconomic efficiency.

The increment in total investment reflects, on the one hand, expectations of solid, sustained domestic market recuperation in the coming years, and on the other, it is a consequence of the liberalization and dynamics of manu-facturing sector exports (see figure 1.11 and table 1.15). The gradual way in which economic reactivation took place

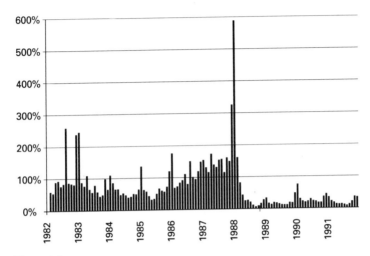

Figure 1.9
Annualized monthly inflation rate (1982–1991)
Source: Banco de México, Indicadores Económicos.

highlights the importance of fiscal restraint during the first stages of the Pact, especially if compared with the over-expansion problems that Brazil, Argentina, and Israel faced in their respective stabilization programs. This contraction becomes indispensable when the balance of payments leaves very little room for movement. Without the primary surplus increase, the Pact would have had a similar fate to the cruzado plan, which saw rapid growth followed by a devaluation and return to hyperinflation (see figure 1.12 and table 1.16).

Wage policy was based on the premise of eliminating the inertial component originating in out-of-phase wage contracts. This has given way to a wage renegotiation atmosphere in which agreements are made on the basis of expected inflation, and not determined in a backward-looking way, which is usually the cause of failure of stabilization

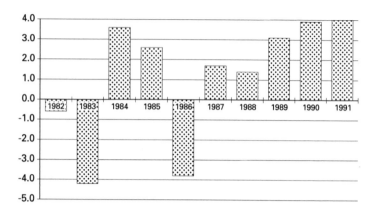

Figure 1.10
Gross domestic product annual rate of growth
Source: INEGI. Estimate for 1991, Criteria for Economic Policy for 1992,
Presidency of the Republic.

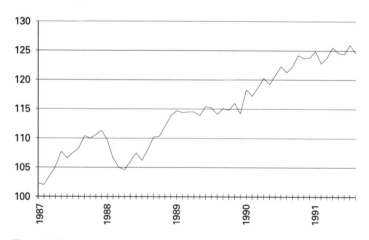

Figure 1.11
Industrial activity (seasonally adjusted index)
Source: Banco de México, Indicadores Económicos.

Table 1.15
Employment and economic activity

		Unemployment rate	Industrial activity index (1980 = 100)
1988	I	3.5	109.3
	II	3.7	107.3
	III	4.0	102.9
	IV	3.2	105.6
1989	I	3.2	112.3
	II	3.0	114.9
	III	3.3	108.3
	IV	2.5	106.5
1990	I	2.5	124.2
	II	2.8	119.8
	III	3.1	116.5
	IV	2.6	112.3
1991	I	2.7	120.9
	II	2.3	122.3
	III	2.9	118.6
	IV	2.6	116.4

Source: Banco de México, Indicadores Económicos, and INEGI, Monthly Survey of Industrial Activity.

programs founded on the fixing of nominal anchors. As time has gone by, contracts have become longer and the recuperation of real wages has been gradually achieved. For instance, by mid-1991, real contractual wages had gone back to their 1987 pre-Pact level, in a context of much faster growth, the expansion of productivity, and exchange rate stability.

The chance to end inertia is the result of greater confidence of all members of society in the economic program.

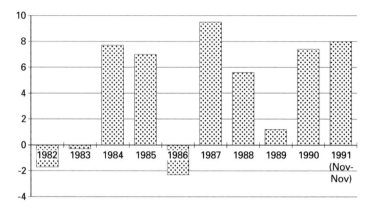

Figure 1.12
Workers insured permanently by IMSS (annual growth rate)
Source: IMSS, Indicadores de Empleo.

Confidence has been regained slowly as a result of the consistency of the macroeconomic and structural reform processes, even when at times there was a great temptation to abandon the program. This is especially true if one looks at the most difficult times in the years during which the preconditions for the success of the Pact were built up, or during the first months of the Pact (see table 1.17).

For instance, in surveying newspaper reports following the first and second rounds of consensus-gathering negotiations, one quickly notes the prevailing sense of uncertainty. As inflation began to come down, however, optimism began to catch up. In the months that have followed, progress in state reform through privatization of larger companies and commercial banks, the completion of the external debt renegotiation, and the prospect of a North American free trade agreement have validated that optimism, which has been translated into lower interest rates

Table 1.16
Annual accumulated growth rate of the manufacturing sector real wage index

	Index (%)		Index (%)
1988	−1.4	*1990*	1.7
February	−1.2	February	1.0
March	2.5	March	−0.2
April	−0.8	April	0.7
May	−1.7	May	1.4
June	−1.5	June	1.5
July	−2.0	July	1.4
August	−2.0	August	1.4
September	−2.3	September	1.2
October	−3.2	October	1.1
November	−3.5	November	1.1
December	−3.3	December	1.1
1989	−1.9	*1991*	3.7
February	−0.9	February	2.0
March	−0.8	March	1.9
April	0.5	April	1.5
May	1.1	May	1.6
June	1.5	June	1.4
July	1.7	July	2.0
August	2.2	August	2.2
September	2.2	September	2.3
October	2.3	October	2.8
November	2.3	November	2.7
December	2.4	December	2.9

Source: prepared with information from Banco de México, Indicadores Económicos, and INEGI, Monthly Survey of Economic Activity.

Table 1.17
Public opinion and the Pact

	First phase	Second phase (% responses)	Third phase
Private sector			
Uncertainty	47.22	28.57	5.88
Government to blame[1]	11.11	7.14	0.00
Optimism	41.67	64.29	94.12
Campesinos and workers			
Uncertainty	71.88	22.22	17.39
Other sectors to blame	18.75	11.11	21.74
Optimism	9.38	66.67	60.87

Source: Created from a random sample of 131 articles published in national newspapers from December 1987 to May 1988.
1. Opinions about whether the Pact would be adequately supported by a consistent fiscal policy.

in spite of increased private investment, and the prospects for a long-run sustainable increase in production and output in a context of exchange rate stability.

Concluding Remarks: Ten Thoughts on Stabilization and Structural Change

As has been briefly described in this chapter, since 1983 Mexico has carried out a profound and comprehensive process of stabilization and structural change. During this time, there have been situations in which it has been possible to make progress without any major setbacks, but there have also been moments when it has been necessary to acknowledge limitations and change course. In the following paragraphs I would like to sum up what has been presented in graphs and tables from a more practical perspective, by reflecting on what the efforts of government and citizens have taught us in the past nine years.

1. *The worst thing to do is nothing.* Some people think that it is better to wait until hyperinflation has set in before trying to stabilize the economy. By then, the argument goes, the dynamics of prices and salaries would be completely linked to the exchange rate, and therefore inflation could be reduced by simply fixing the parity and applying the corresponding strict monetary policy, instead of having to apply a wide array of structural change measures to reinforce the budget and make the necessary monetary adjustment. The Latin American experience of the 1980s, however, has shown that the deeper the crisis, the more difficult it is to get out because economic disorder not only paralyzes all productive activities, it also erodes the trust among government, entrepreneurs, workers, and farmers.

A sound and permanent recovery needs to be based on strong democratic institutions through which the entire process of modernization of the economy will be studied and implemented. This is why the institutions have to be protected from the effects of confusion and mistrust. Therefore, once a problem is detected, the first decision to be made is how to correct it before it is too late.

2. *Vital to the success of the reform program is the quality and commitment of key public servants.* Without well-trained politicians and economists ready to put their minds to work on the solution of very complex problems—and with the will and unity to take the necessary decisions—no modernization program could be successful. It is indispensable to have top-grade people who are also convinced of the philosophy of stabilization and structural change in the areas

of budget control, domestic and international trade, privatization, industrial regulation, social security, labor management, social development, taxation, and financial policy.

3. There is no macroeconomic stability without a deep and permanent reform of public finances. The experience of the last few years has shown us that fiscal orthodoxy is a necessary condition for restoring stability and economic growth; however, we have also learned that it is not sufficient as long as there are persistent structural disequilibria.

It is very important to resist the temptation to believe that a program can still be successful with an insufficient and/or temporary fiscal adjustment, as long as it is complemented with income policies of price and wage restraints. Sooner rather than later such a program will result in a worsening in the external accounts combined with generalized shortages, which will eventually force a devaluation, price liberalization, and the reindexation of the economy, at the enormous cost of the loss of credibility on the authorities.

Not only must the fiscal adjustment be profound, it must also be permanent. It is imperative to avoid transitory adjustments, which have only a cosmetic effect on the statistics. Permanent actions, such as the bankruptcy of inefficient public enterprises, must be taken to send the message that the authorities have the political courage to move ahead with the economic program until the objectives are reached. In conclusion, a sizeable primary surplus is a precondition that has to be met before beginning to talk about the correction of inflationary inertia and the selection of nominal anchors for stabilization.

4. Stabilization and structural change have to be viewed as integral elements of a single strategy. Aggregate demand and structural change policies have some elements that complement and reinforce each other, and others that are contradictory. This is why it is essential to coordinate them in the design as well as the implementation phases of the economic program.

This point can be illustrated with two concrete cases. For example, one of the indispensable measures for the rationalization of public finances is the elimination of subsidies. When these are removed, however, the prices of final goods increase, reviving pressure leading toward indexation of the economy. In these circumstances it is clear that timing is important: the subsidies will have to disappear gradually to be consistent with inflation targets, but the process has to be uninterrupted to avoid sacrificing the fiscal balance.

In the same way there will be cases in which both types of policies work in the same direction: for example, the elimination of trade barriers and the reduction of tariffs not only eliminate distortions and lead toward a more efficient allocation of resources, but can also work to stabilize the prices of tradeables and therefore to achieve overall inflation targets.

5. *The worst defect of an economic program is negligence.* The speed with which one moves is crucial, because it will take several months before the adjustment efforts begin to show some benefits, whereas the costs show up immediately. Lengthy proceedings slowly wear out the political patience of the population and force the authorities to make concessions that jeopardize the entire program.

In addition, some things will inevitably take time. For example, the privatization of enterprises does not consist only of announcing that a firm is for sale: one has to make a careful appraisal of the business, design the sales strategy, look for clients, and follow step by step the procedures as established by law. When there is so much to do and so much to learn, time becomes extremely valuable.

6. *Start at the beginning.* Common sense suggests a natural order of things. A stabilization program has to start from strong fundamentals such as a manageable operational deficit, an adequate real exchange rate, and a level of reserves and/or net transfers congruent with the sustainable targets of long-term growth.

At first, the policy of correction in the public finances has to consist of across-the-board cuts, because at the beginning there is so much "extra fat" in every area that it is unlikely that anything essential will be affected. Only after this first step has been taken may the government proceed with selective spending reductions.

The same is true of the process of privatization, which has to start with small firms, not only to allow the government to learn how to sell them, but also to break the bureaucratic inertia of the years of overexpansion and crisis. In addition, as the stabilization program advances, the assets of parastatal firms will be increasing in value, making it possible to sell the large ones at a better price.

7. *Consistency plus credibility equals confidence.* Restoring and maintaining the credibility of the authorities is essential to strengthening the confidence of the people. To be credible one has to set (clearly, from the very beginning) macroeconomic objectives and determine the role of the state in the economy; once this is done one has to understand that there is no way back.

Credibility is not a gift—it has to be earned. It is built up one step at a time and supported by facts, and by consistency. Even more, credibility is never owned; it is rented, because it can be taken away at any time.

The period covered by the agreements reached in the negotiations of the social pact for stability extended for only one month at the beginning. Later on they lasted two or three months, and now they take a year. It took some time before people began to believe. Credibility is earned in the most difficult moments, and not when the winds work in your favor. When the temptation arises to reindex the economy and retreat from what has been achieved in fiscal adjustment, but the authorities hold firm, that is the moment at which people realize that their government is willing to meet its commitment.

Experience has shown that the costs of policy inconsistency are very high in the long run. We cannot afford to forget that, as Keynes said almost seventy years ago, expectations play a crucial role in macroeconomic performance. This is even more clearly indicated by the vicious circles of capital flight and recession in Latin America: capital flies away because there is no internal stability, but there is no stability because capital flies away.

8. The government cannot go it alone. Negotiation among sectors is necessary to make the program work. A government cannot stop inflation and restore healthy growth on its own: along with fiscal sacrifice, real wages and operating margins of firms must also go through an orderly adjustment, which would be impossible without a negotiated consensus.

Whenever possible, the authorities must communicate with the various sectors to tell them what is being attempted, hear their comments, and outline for them the costs and benefits of the measures being taken. When there is any difficulty, policy makers must make sure that they know how the problem came about, the extent of the damage, and what is going to be done to solve it. They must resist the temptation to cheat with statistics or hide something important, not only because this is the morally right thing to do, but because in pluralistic and democratic societies everything comes to light sooner or later.

9. *Be fair.* The public may not understand every technical detail that is provided, but they have all the time in the world to realize if one sector is being favored over another. Therefore, fairness is paramount: the adjustment program will demand sacrifices on the part of the government, workers, entrepreneurs, and foreign creditors. The burden has to be distributed among them fairly, which does not necessarily mean equally. Being fair means protecting those who are more vulnerable to the crisis, even at the risk of being uneven. Neither should advantage be taken of any group. For example, the government cannot raise taxes without giving anything in exchange. If revenues are going to be higher, people have the right to improved services.

10. *It is easier to lower inflation from 200 percent to 20 percent than it is to take it from 20 percent to international levels.* Looking at the experience of stabilization in other developing countries, as well as at our own experience, it seems possible to succeed in the attempt to go from hyperinflation to more moderate levels. However, no one has succeeded in taking inflation to between 6 percent and 4 percent. The challenge remains to make this final transition while strengthening long-term growth prospects for the economy and ensuring an improvement in the standard of living of every segment of the population.

2   Financial and Fiscal Reform

An interesting interplay takes place between financial systems and tax systems in an economy. On the one hand, it is via taxes, inflation, and voluntary savings that most investment—and therefore most of the expansion of production and employment—are financed. On the other hand, taxes and interest rates redistribute the nation's wealth from one generation to another, or from one income group to another. Therefore, when dealing with financial and fiscal matters, one cannot afford to think only in terms of macroeconomic balances; it is also extremely important to be aware of the social impact of each policy decision.[1]

The awareness among economists of a link between distribution and growth is nothing new, but the understanding of the way both variables interact through fiscal and financial channels is changing. More than a century ago, the Marxian theory argued that growth came about because labor was paid a wage below the value of the output it generated. This created a surplus which could keep growing—or reproducing itself, in Marx's words—to the extent that reinvesting it would increase the productivity of labor without necessarily bringing about an increase in real wages. In the twentieth century, the relationship between

distribution and growth was revisited, shifting the emphasis from what happened in the labor market to a more
normative view. For instance, the 1950s Kaldorian theory
of growth stated that to achieve a high rate of output expansion, it was necessary to redistribute income from the high-
propensity-to-spend groups (generally workers or low-
income people) to high-propensity-to-save groups. Then a
more uneven distribution was an inevitable by-product of
a successful industrialization program.

The experience of the last twenty-five years in developing
countries, however, has proved the contrary to what the
above theories were able to predict. A worsening distribution of output and wealth not only failed to translate into
faster and more sustainable growth in every case,[2] but as
more recent studies[3] have shown, those countries with
poorer distributions of income grew more slowly on average and appear to have been much more vulnerable to
external shocks (see figure 2.1).

Mexico can be considered one of the cases in which
regressive income distribution has been associated with
poor growth performance. After having followed a strategy
based on tax exemptions and privileges to infant industries
and other "high-priority sectors," a repressed financial sector was expected to provide an inexpensive and noninflationary way of financing the budget deficit.[4] As a result,
the economy ended up with an institutional framework
incapable of responding to unfavorable external shocks. It
could raise neither taxes nor interest rates, and thus had to
rely on inflationary financing and/or on the contraction of
aggregate demand. When the government could not bring
spending down far enough, the economy had to experience
devaluations and drops in real wages.[5]

The facts have proved that a poor distribution of income
and a rigid financial and fiscal system is a dangerous com-

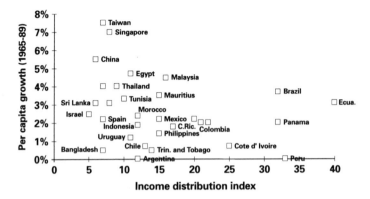

Figure 2.1
International comparisons of income distribution and growth
Source: World Bank Development Report, (1991), The Index of Income
Inequality is the result of multiplying the proportion of income earned by
the two deciles of highest income and the two deciles of lowest income.

bination and is incompatible with long-term growth. In such an environment, adjustment efforts can only reduce real wages to a certain minimum level. After that, the only alternative is to have more inflation, which, once it has entered the double-digit range, introduces extremely high costs in terms of the allocative efficiency of markets, economic incentives needed to increase investment, and further inequity of income distribution.[6]

The above line of reasoning played an important role in setting up the standards for Mexico's recent adjustment. This chapter explains the reforms in finance, income, and expenditure policies. The review of the fiscal and financial reform in Mexico is made from the dual perspective of growth and social justice. For example, section 1 looks at financial reform from two angles: the role of financial innovation and liberalization in generating further savings and allowing prices and quantities to share in the response to external shocks, and the role of development banking in supporting a new industrialization strategy based on greater access of small and micro-entrepreneurs to credit. The report on fiscal reform contained in section 2 shows how tax revenues were increased through a much more even distribution of the tax burden across sectors and income groups, as opposed to higher tax rates. Finally, section 3 describes the social spending program of President Salinas de Gortari in terms of the assistance it provides to people below the poverty line and the channeling of resources into productive activities.

1 Financial Reform

Before attempting to talk about the desirable characteristics of a financial system, and therefore about the direction of financial reform, it is important to acknowledge that the institutions and regulatory framework of the financial sector can have a significant impact on growth performance and economic development in at least the following three ways:

a. Financial institutions can magnify or buffer internal and external shocks to the economy. The way in which they are legally allowed to operate limits how far monetary and fiscal authorities can go in carrying out an effective countercyclical policy.

b. To the extent that growth requires investment, and investment requires savings, financial intermediaries can obstruct or facilitate this process by providing the instruments for people to save and by channeling these savings into activities with attractive rates of return.

c. Due to the economies of scale in financial services and the cost of information in developing countries, credit is usually not within the reach of small enterprises. This means that profitable projects are left at the margin, and that incomplete financial markets can have a very regressive impact on income distribution.

Because of this complexity, a successful financial reform has to be seen as a package of measures that neither begins and nor ends with the fixing or freeing of interest rates. It had to include measures to back the creation of new financial instruments and redefine the role of development banks and commercial institutions, as well as fiscal and monetary policies in the new regulatory environment.

To get as clear a view as possible of the economic and social dimensions of the financial reform, I would like to discuss in detail each of these three financial factors in economic development. The first two concern how a reform can contribute to economic efficiency, and the third addresses the social impact of financial institutions.

1.1 The Macroeconomic Dimension of the Financial Reform

1.1.1 Financial Structure and Macroeconomic Stability in the Mexican Experience

The modern history of the Mexican financial system began in 1925 with the enactment of the law creating the Banco de México (central bank) and the framework for what would come to be a three-tier financial system. On one level were the commercial banks, whose main function was to receive short-term deposits and give short-term credits to enterprises, while financing the credit needs of the state. The second group consisted of the auxiliary institutions (insurance, bonding, and warehouse companies) and the so-called *financieras* that captured long-term savings coming sometimes from banks, but mainly from the public, which in turn would be used to provide long-term financing to either enterprises or consumers. Finally, the third category corresponded to the development banks, whose funds come primarily from public resources in the form of budgetary allocations, foreign resources, or credits received from the Banco de México. In turn, these funds are used to finance small enterprises, private farmers and *ejidatarios,* or long-term loans like mortgages.

The private credit institutions were regulated by the Ministry of Finance and the Banco de México mainly through the use of three instruments.[7] First, there was the legal reserve requirement, which took the form of compulsory credit to the public sector at no cost or low rates. Second, there were quantitative controls to credit under a scheme known as "selective credit quotas." Under this scheme, intermediaries had the obligation to keep a given proportion of their lending portfolios assigned to certain sectors, such as agriculture, or to small- and medium-sized enterprises. Third, both borrowing and lending rates were set by the authorities and usually remained fixed for very long periods. The stock market played a very limited role within this framework. There was basically no room for open market operations, and therefore monetary policy was carried out essentially through the Banco de México's financing of the public sector and through the adjustment of the reserve requirement for intermediaries.

This simple, specialized, and regulated financial setting worked quite well during the first years of the Mexican industrialization experience. As can be seen in table 2.1,[8] during the 1950s and 1960s the government relied very little on inflationary financing. This allowed the economy to advance in terms of financial intermediation, in a context of price and exchange rate stability and rapid output growth.

During the 1970s, the authorities initiated a series of limited reforms to the financial system. The idea was to provide greater flexibility to interest rates and make bank operations more efficient, but these reforms did not change the essence of financial intermediation in Mexico. In 1974,[9] legislation was introduced to increase the range of operations of commercial banks, which from that time on would be known as "banca multiple" or "multiple banks." Under the new scheme, the same institution could offer specialized services, such as deposits, savings, mortgages, and trust fund management, that had previously been provided by specialized banks.[10] In the same year Congress passed the Stock Market Act, which created the legal framework for the development of nonbank financial intermediaries, while establishing the National Securities and Exchange Commission to supervise and regulate the operations in capital and money markets.

On the financial innovation side, in May 1977 it was decided to diversify the deposit instruments offered to the public by the banking sector. The most interesting change was the introduction of deposit accounts with predetermined withdrawal dates, which would pay higher yields. This time interest rates would not be fixed, but the Banco de México would still be able to determine the maximum return on these instruments.

In spite of these reforms, the events of the last twenty years showed that the system was too rigid to function properly in times of moderate to high inflation, and that the delay in introducing the necessary reforms of the financial sector decisively aggravated both the dynamics and the extent of the crisis. Monetary control became increasingly limited by the fact that the minimum reserve requirement in an inflationary environment—exacerbated by the rise in the borrowing requirements of the public sector and the more limited capacity to obtain funds abroad—came to be determined mostly by the evolution of the deficit, therefore reducing its margins to effectively regulate the quantity of money.

Maintaining a fixed exchange rate when inflation accelerated at the beginning of the 1970s not only put pressure on the balance of payments as the real exchange rate appreciated. Since interest rates were not allowed to respond to higher inflation (and to the eventual depreciation of the peso), the process of capital flight was also fueled, making the external disequilibria even worse (see table 2.1 and figure 2.2).

In addition, by carefully reexamining the events leading to the 1976 and 1982 crises in terms of financial markets, it has been established[11] that quantitative credit controls (and the combination of fixed interest rates and the exchange rate) were closely linked to the paradoxical and simultaneous process of private capital flight and private foreign borrowing in the months before the devaluations. Because the banks had to ration credit without governmental intervention (because people were taking their money out of the banks to place it abroad) and dollarization,[12] firms had to borrow abroad simply to stay in business (see figure 2.3).

At the beginning of the 1980s, it became clear that the existing financial arrangement was not only contributing to a volatile environment, but also that financial institutions had been weakened by the combination of regulations and macroeconomic conditions. For example, insurance companies had been required to keep their reserves in instruments that paid a fixed nominal interest rate of less than 5 percent throughout the years of high inflation, translating

Table 2.1
Mexico's financial indicators, 1951–1991 (%)

	GDP growth	Inflation	Nominal deposit rates[1]	Financial deepening[2]	Inflation tax (% GDP)	Net credit Banxico to govt.[3]
1951	7.69	23.97	8.00	16.74	2.21	0.7
1952	3.94	4.00	8.00	15.74	0.66	0.5
1953	0.29	−1.92	8.00	18.79	0.66	1.0
1954	9.99	7.84	8.00	16.77	1.89	0.7
1955	8.50	14.55	8.00	16.43	1.11	−1.7
1956	6.88	5.29	8.00	15.64	1.17	0.0
1957	7.55	6.03	8.00	14.72	0.68	0.4
1958	5.31	3.32	8.00	14.23	0.76	1.5
1959	3.01	0.00	8.00	14.85	0.57	0.3
1960	8.11	5.50	8.00	18.21	0.38	0.5
1961	4.92	0.00	8.00	18.93	0.46	1.1
1962	4.69	1.30	8.00	20.72	1.28	0.7
1963	8.00	2.15	8.00	22.31	1.63	0.2
1964	11.67	5.04	8.00	22.61	2.36	0.2
1965	6.50	0.80	8.00	23.93	1.23	0.8
1966	6.92	1.98	8.00	25.98	1.24	0.8
1967	6.29	0.78	8.00	28.18	1.72	−0.1
1968	8.14	1.93	8.00	29.76	1.72	0.2
1969	6.32	1.68	8.00	32.08	1.46	1.3
1970	6.91	6.95	8.00	33.97	1.24	0.2
1971	4.19	5.26	8.00	35.08	2.29	−0.2
1972	8.47	5.00	8.00	35.88	2.39	3.7
1973	8.43	12.04	12.91	33.46	2.56	3.3
1974	6.10	23.75	12.44	30.34	3.12	3.7
1975	5.63	11.20	11.97	31.46	3.92	3.0
1976	4.23	27.20	12.12	28.84	3.68	1.8
1977	3.45	20.70	14.04	22.04	3.90	12.8

Table 2.1 (continued)

	GDP growth	Inflation	Nominal deposit rates[1]	Finan-cial deep-ening[2]	Inflation tax (% GDP)	Net credit Banxico to govt.[3]
1978	8.25	16.20	15.88	24.86	3.58	3.7
1979	9.16	20.00	17.52	26.00	4.31	5.1
1980	8.33	29.80	24.25	32.72	4.88	6.0
1981	7.95	28.70	31.81	35.34	5.51	5.9
1982	−0.55	98.80	46.12	38.75	10.00	17.5
1983	−5.28	80.80	56.44	35.56	6.72	11.3
1984	3.68	59.20	47.54	37.87	5.91	8.8
1985	2.78	63.70	65.66	32.84	1.78	9.9
1986	−3.53	105.70	95.33	39.16	3.41	13.6
1987	1.70	159.20	104.30	42.39	3.29	11.3
1988	1.30	51.60	45.48	34.20	1.53	6.1
1989	3.10	19.70	40.11	39.53	0.43	1.0
1990	4.40	29.90	29.20	44.30	1.22	2.9
1991	3.60	18.80	19.90	45.49	0.66	0.0

Source: Prepared with data from Banco de México.
1. Housing bond rates before 1973. After 1973 is the average cost of funds of the banking system.
2. (M4/GDP); using along the series the more comprehensive definition of money at the time.
3. As a fraction of GDP; includes the public financial sector.

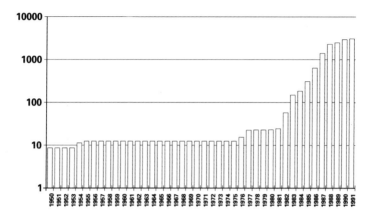

Figure 2.2
Nominal exchange rate (pesos per dollar)
Source: Banco de México, Indicadores Económicos. 1) Period average.

into a serious and rapid decapitalization of the sector. Also, banks had been hit by the devaluations, dollarization, and capital flight, so by the time they were nationalized in 1982, they were already in a precarious situation.

In conclusion, the facts suggest that as soon as the fiscal discipline of the years of the *desarrollo estabilizador* was broken, the financial system had to be made more flexible to prevent capital flight and the deterioration in the balance sheets of financial intermediaries and to avoid the need for inflationary financing, while giving the authorities a clearer idea of the real limits of deficit financing of economic growth.

1.1.2 Financial Policies and the Promotion of Savings in the Mexican Experience
Apart from their role as a buttress to short-term stability, financial institutions carry out the task of collecting savings and channeling them into productive projects. In this

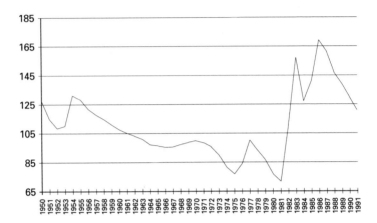

Figure 2.3
Real exchange rate (index)
Source: Prepared with data from Banco de México, Indicadores Económicos. 1) Defined as R = Nominal Exchange Rate in pesos per dollar *
External Price Level/Domestic Price Level. Elaborated using the price level
of the USA as external price level. Higher values of the index mean a
relative depreciation of the peso. End of the period.

respect, there has been a serious debate as to what extent
financial institutions can actually influence the savings rate.
Proponents of life-cycle theories[13] believe that the main
incentives to save are linked more to the age structure of
the population than to financial institutions. Another point
of debate has to do with the question of the relation between
domestic savings and domestic investment. The answer to
both questions depends very much on the characteristics
of each country; in the case of Mexico, long-term experience
strongly suggests that changes in the financial sector can
actually affect not only the levels of financial intermediation
but the overall level of savings. In addition, it has also been
found that increases in private and public savings can

actually contribute to growth, as they are linked to higher levels of domestic investment.[14]

Compared with the countries with higher rates of growth, Mexican savings and investment rates are low. For instance, whereas the Pacific basin countries invest around 30 percent of GDP, in Mexico this number is barely above 20 percent. This figure also seems small when compared with the rates of investment achieved during the years of faster growth, when the rate of gross fixed capital formation reached 27percent of GDP. Therefore, to sustain an acceptable rate of expansion of per capita income, one should expect some improvement in the rate of savings through additional fiscal discipline and more private domestic and external savings (see table 2.2).

To get an idea of what would have to be done to increase savings, it is necessary to look in some detail at the factors affecting the performance of private savings[15] in Mexico for

Table 2.2
International comparisons on saving and investment rates, 1980–1989 (%)

	Per capita GDP growth	Savings/ GNP	Investment/ GNP
Developed countries	1.5	22.3	22.1
Less developed countries			
Africa	−3.7	10.1	15.1
Far East	6.4	30.2	29.9
Middle East	2.9	18.4	22.4
Latin America	−2.2	16.9	18.8
Mexico	−2.0	21.1	20.7

Source: World Bank, *World Development Report*, several issues, and from Cuentas Nacionales, SPP.

the past forty years.[16] The first important observation is that private voluntary savings have not been crowded out by forced noninflationary forms of savings. In other words, in Mexico taxes and Social Security contributions have been complementary to other forms of private savings. One reason for this may be that a vast majority of the population has lacked access to instruments through which to save for retirement and insure against a variety of risks. Therefore, what has been recorded as voluntary savings is related to other reasons for saving, such as precautionary motives, or in the case of firms, self-financing.[17] Because people have not been able to make intertemporal and intergenerational transfers through the financial system, they have had to rely on other means, such as having more children to look after them when they get old, or by buying durables, which are certainly not registered as savings.

A second and closely related factor is that voluntary savings respond positively to financial innovation and financial intermediation (captured by the degree of financial deepening[18]), which also reflects the degree to which financial markets are still very fragmented. There is evidence that owing to the lack of instruments for hedging against inflation and exchange rate risks, to mention but a few types of risk, people prefer to buy a durable good. Therefore, the creation of new financial instruments can also help promote savings.

A third element is related to the degree of income inequality. Using data on the factor distribution of income[19] as a proxy for personal income,[20] it was found that in contrast to the Kaldorian view, widening the participation of labor income in national income contributes to an increase in voluntary savings (see table 2.3). Finally, there is evidence that negative real interest rates depress the level of volun-

Table 2.3
Investment and savings performance in Mexico, 1950–1990 (% of GDP)

	Invest-ment[1]	External savings	Domestic savings	Private savings[2]	Public sec. savings[3]	Pub. sect. balance	Public invest-ment
1950	13.5	−3.2	16.7	10.8	5.9	−0.2	6.1
1951	14.4	3.2	11.2	6.3	4.9	−0.3	5.2
1952	16.9	3.1	13.8	6.9	6.9	1.4	5.5
1953	15.2	2.8	12.4	8.3	4.1	−0.9	5.0
1954	17.1	3.5	13.6	8.9	4.7	−1.0	5.7
1955	18.1	0.0	18.1	13.4	4.7	−0.3	5.0
1956	20.2	2.3	17.9	13.7	4.2	−0.4	4.6
1957	18.4	3.9	14.5	10.4	4.1	−0.8	4.9
1958	17.4	3.9	13.5	9.2	4.3	−0.7	5.0
1959	16.5	2.2	14.3	10.0	4.3	−0.6	4.9
1960	20.1	3.5	16.6	11.8	4.8	−0.8	5.6
1961	18.1	2.7	15.4	9.7	5.7	−0.7	6.4
1962	16.5	1.8	14.7	9.0	5.7	−0.4	6.1
1963	19.4	1.4	18.0	12.2	5.8	−1.3	7.1
1964	20.9	2.5	18.4	11.3	7.1	−0.8	7.9
1965	20.6	2.3	18.3	13.7	4.6	−0.8	5.4
1966	22.6	2.2	20.4	15.8	4.6	−1.1	5.7
1967	21.9	2.5	19.4	14.5	4.9	−2.1	7.0
1968	20.8	2.9	17.9	12.9	5.0	−1.9	6.9
1969	21.1	2.4	18.7	13.7	5.0	−2.0	7.0
1970	21.1	3.3	17.8	14.6	3.2	−3.4	6.6
1971	20.2	2.4	17.8	15.5	2.3	−2.3	4.6
1972	20.3	2.2	18.1	16.7	1.4	−4.5	5.9
1973	21.4	2.8	18.6	17.7	0.9	−6.3	7.2
1974	23.2	4.5	18.7	18.2	0.5	−6.7	7.2
1975	23.7	5.0	18.7	19.3	−0.6	−9.3	8.7
1976	22.3	4.1	18.2	19.4	−1.2	−9.1	7.9
1977	22.8	1.9	20.9	19.6	1.3	−6.3	7.6
1978	23.5	2.6	20.9	18.4	2.5	−6.2	8.7
1979	26.0	3.6	22.4	19.7	2.7	−7.1	9.8

Table 2.3 (continued)

	Invest-ment[1]	External savings	Domestic savings	Private savings[2]	Public sec. savings[3]	Pub. sect. balance	Public invest-ment
1980	27.1	5.8	21.3	19.2	2.1	−7.5	9.6
1981	27.3	6.7	20.6	21.8	−1.2	−14.1	12.9
1982	22.9	3.6	19.3	26.0	−6.7	−16.9	10.2
1983	20.8	−4.5	25.3	26.4	−1.1	−8.6	7.5
1984	19.9	−2.7	22.6	24.4	−1.8	−8.5	6.7
1985	21.2	−0.8	22.0	25.5	−3.5	−9.6	6.1
1986	18.2	1.3	16.9	26.8	−9.9	−15.9	6.0
1987	19.2	−3.0	22.2	32.7	−10.5	−16.0	5.5
1988	21.2	1.0	20.2	28.2	−8.0	−12.4	4.4
1989	23.0	2.3	20.7	22.3	−1.6	−5.5	3.9
1990	24.3	2.6	21.7	20.2	1.5	−4.0	5.0

Source: Banco de México, Indicadores Económicos, and DGPH, Ministry of Finance.
1. Gross fixed investment plus changes in inventories.
2. Defined here as the difference between domestic savings (investment-external savings) and public savings.
3. Government deficit minus public sector investment.

tary savings. In summary, the financial policies and the financial system, at least in a country with the characteristics of Mexico, can therefore have a significant impact on long-term voluntary savings. A policy of positive real interest rates, combined with the creation of new financial instruments and an active fiscal policy to collect more taxes and improve income distribution, can promote further savings, investment, and growth.

1.1.3 The Financial Reform (1983–1991)

In light of what has been said in the two previous sections, it could be claimed that an effective program of reform for Mexico, from the standpoint of both short- and medium-term macroeconomic stability and the long-term promotion of savings, had to modify financial institutions in at least the following five aspects:

a. Financial liberalization: replacing a system based on the combination of quantitative restrictions to credit and regulated interest rates with one in which monetary policy is carried out mainly through open market operations, and where interest rates are allowed to respond rapidly to internal and external shocks.

b. Financial innovation: creating instruments that would make it possible for people to hedge against inflation and exchange rate uncertainty and make intergenerational and intertemporal transfers more efficiently.

c. Strengthening financial intermediaries: taking measures to allow credit institutions to reach a larger number of customers and give them access to a variety of services at the lowest possible cost, while maintaining their own financial strength.

d. Privatizing commercial banks.

e. Financing the government deficit: instead of shifting the financing from compulsory reserve requirements to credits from the central bank, there should be an increased allocation of noninflationary debt instruments through credit markets.

In what follows I would like to describe briefly how the actual modernization of the financial system has taken place in each of these five areas during the last nine years.

a. Financial Liberalization

As has been already stated, between the 1950s and early 1980s, control over credit aggregates was carried out essentially through quantitative controls on the intermediaries by the imposition of reserve requirements, selective credit quotas, borrowing interest rates predetermined by the Banco de México—in many cases upon instructions from the Ministry of Finance and not by current market conditions. The departure from this rigid scheme began in 1978, when the authorities issued the Certificates of the Treasury (CETES) as a first attempt to develop a money market. However, the initial operations were very small and lacked a secondary market, and yields were fixed by the authorities. It was not until the last quarter of 1982 that paticipants in CETES auctions were free to present their bids in terms of amounts and yields. The primary and secondary market developed rapidly thereafter, and the auction system continued to be gradually improved (see figure 2.4).

Especially since autumn 1988, the monetary authorities have tried to follow a pragmatic approach regarding interest

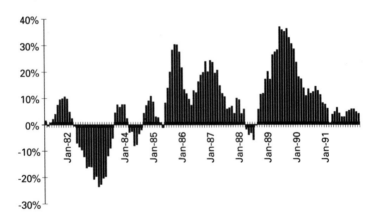

Figure 2.4
Annualized real yield of 30-day Treasury certificates
Source: Elaborated with the information from Banco de México, Indicadores Económicos.

rates by letting the market play its role, while targeting on the level of inflation and international reserves. Then, in spite of the enormous outlays implied by the service of the domestic debt and the temptation to curb soaring interest rates in times of volatile external conditions and unfavorable expectations, the government's policy remained focused on creating a reputation of monetary and fiscal prudence. Even though real interest rates stayed above 30 percent per year, the response in terms of financial savings was not immediate. In fact, for most of the time between 1983 and 1989, the velocity of the most comprehensive definition of money (M4) remained at its highest post-devaluation level. However, it would be fair to say that this in itself was not a failure, because the main objective of stopping capital flight and developing a new financial culture was being achieved. Finally, after the favorable news of the debt renegotiation, the privatization of commercial banks and the beginning of negotiations of a free trade agreement with Canada and the United States, financial intermediation increased very fast as the process of capital repatriation picked up (see figure 2.5).

Regarding the gradual elimination of quantitative controls to credit, the second phase in the process of financial liberalization started in 1988, beginning with the elimination of "credit quotas" to high-priority sectors and continuing with the removal of compulsory reserve requirements. It must be mentioned that since 1976 commercial banks have been allowed to collect resources from the public by means of direct checking and savings deposits, as well as certificates of deposit and promissory notes. Given the differences in the nature of the operation of these two sources of bank liabilities, the first liberalization measure consisted

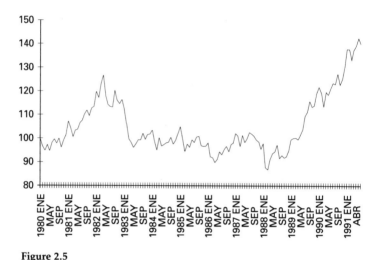

Figure 2.5
Financial deepening (M4/GDP)
Source: Elaborated with information from Banco de México, Indicadores
Económicos, and INEGI, Monthly Survey of Industrial Activity.

of eliminating the quota restrictions on resources coming
from these so-called nontraditional bank instruments. In
this way, starting in October 1988, only bank balances
linked to checking and savings accounts faced limitations
on the percentage that should be channeled into "high-
priority areas" and development banks on top of the compulsory reserve requirement. The rest of the bank liabilities
were freed from the *selective credit mechanism*, and the previous regime of *minimum reserve* of direct credits to the
government was replaced by a "liquidity requirement,"
which imposed only the obligation to keep 30 percent of
the portfolio in interest-bearing government paper. In April
1989 the reform was extended to traditional time deposits,
and finally in August to checking accounts. Simultaneously,

banks were authorized to pay interest on checking accounts.

In this way, by August the authorities had gotten rid of the selective credit mechanism and were somewhat prepared to phase out what was left of the minimum reserve system. This decision was put into effect on September 11, when it was thought that the preconditions had been satisfied to lift all forms of credit control without incurring adverse macroeconomic effects. These preconditions implied having strong public finances and a reasonably well-working market for government instruments. Otherwise, lifting a source of "forced financing" and of monetary control could introduce very strong inflationary pressures if the burden of government financing were to shift to the central bank. To ensure a smooth transition to the new regime, along with the notification to all banks that the obligatory "liquidity coefficient" of 30 percent would no longer apply, the authorities put in place an ad hoc 10 year variable-rate government note to be used and traded among banks to meet their needs for voluntary reserves. With the implementation of these decisions, the process of liberalization from a repressed financial system to a transparent market-based setting was essentially completed. These changes represent a big first step into a totally different conception of the role and use of financial institutions in the financing of economic development in Mexico.

b. Financial Innovation
Another crucial task consists of creating new financial instruments to help people transfer resources over time, finance their needs at the lowest possible cost, and hedge against a variety of risks—all with the assurance that market participants are being carefully monitored by the authori-

ties. As a consequence of the decision of the government to develop the markets of CETES, the participants in the market, especially *casas de bolsa* (brokerage houses), had the opportunity to grow. Later on they could look for more business by promoting the use of other private sector securities which, although they had been contemplated for a long time, had not played any significant role in the process of financial intermediation.

More as a result of the experience with nontraditional instruments than any important change in regulation, between 1983 and 1991 the savings and funding alternatives have multiplied, and with them the range of operations that can be conducted in the money and capital markets. Whereas ten years ago most of the intermediation took place via banking instruments such as *preestablecidos* (defined below) and savings and checking accounts, now government, individuals, and enterprises—domestic and foreign—carry out their financial operations with a variety of instruments, the most important of which are the following:

i) Banking sector instruments

Cuenta maestra	Provides the service of an ordinary checking account; however, funds are automatically placed in an investment trust account, thus furnishing both liquidity and interest.
Preestablecidos	Deposits that may be withdrawn only on specific days of the week or month, and have fixed interest rates during the period.

Non-negotiable CDs	Issued with a maturity of almost any number of days from 30 to 725, and yield a monthly interest rate that is fixed at the time the deposit is made. They can be denominated in pesos or U.S. dollars.
Promissory notes	Issued in terms of one, three, and six months, with an interest rate fixed at the time of deposit and paid at maturity. These notes can be traded through the stock exchange.

ii) Public sector securities

Treasury certificates	Treasury bills sold at a discount during weekly auctions, with maturities of 28, 91, 182, and 364 days. These are the most important money market instrument.
Pagafes	Dollar-denominated treasury bills, with maturities of 28, 180, and 364 days.
Bondes	Development bonds issued with one- or two-year maturities, denominated in pesos.
Ceplatas	Certificates of participation in a trust fund that holds silver bars. Each certificate is equivalent to 100 ounces, and they are traded on the stock market.

Tesobono	Treasury notes with one- and three-month maturities, with returns indexed to the market exchange rate against the dollar.
Ajustabono	Instrument with three- to five-year maturities with returns indexed to the consumer price index.

iii) Private sector securities

Bankers acceptances	Short-term letters of credit issued at a discount by private firms and guaranteed by commercial banks.
Commercial paper	Nonguaranteed negotiable note with a maturity of up to 180 days.
Obligaciones	Bonds with maturities of more than three years. They can be unsecured *(quirografarias)* or mortgage-backed *(hipotecarias)*.

iv) Instruments for foreign investment in the stock market

Free subscription shares	"Series B" shares of firms listed in the Mexican stock exchange, which can be bought by foreign investors. They carry the same corporate and patrimonial rights as shares bought by Mexican nationals, but are subject to the limits dictated by the National Foreign Investment Commission.

Neutral funds	Trust funds whose assets are "Series A" shares of listed companies (exclusive for Mexicans). Foreign investors receive a Certificate of Ordinary Participation (CPO) issued by the trust manager. These certificates carry only patrimonial rights.

c. Strengthening Financial Intermediaries

Some time ago, Carlos Díaz Alejandro,[21] when talking about financial institutions, said that one could not afford to think of financial markets as markets for chickens or apples, because even though one will always find the familiar supply and demand—and hopefully an equilibrium price level—the consequences of poor regulation in financial markets are far more serious, as they determine the fate of banks, insurance companies, and the stock market.

It would be an exaggeration to say that banks have to be under state control, and certainly our experience leads us to think that private sector banking can be more efficient than public sector banking in traditional commercial activities. However, it would take us to the other equally unsatisfactory extreme to claim that banks can be chartered without a serious screening of who is getting the right to operate with everybody else's money.

To strike a balance that would avoid the errors of the past, it was essential to establish a set of rules that guaranteed the right to enter the market, and at the same time provided clarity and confidence for those who participate in it. This would translate into laws that impose restrictions on who can be a financial intermediary, on how banks will interact with their clients, and on how, while taking advantage of the economies of scale in financial services, to ensure the existence of a competitive environment. Last but not least, the new rules for credit institutions had to allow financial intermediaries such as insurance companies, which had been neglected during the years of overexpansion and crisis, to once again play an important role in the savings and financing process.

Between December 1989 and mid-1990, Congress passed a number of reforms contained in the Credit Institutions Act and authorized changes in related laws to permit the creation of financial groups.

THE CREDIT INSTITUTIONS ACT.   The new Credit Institutions Act regulates banking, as well as the activities of the rest of the financial intermediaries, and establishes the terms under which the government exercises control over the banking system. Under the previous legislation, banking was considered a public service; private parties thus provided banking services under a concession discretionally granted by the ministry of finance. After the nationalization of the banks in 1982, they were transformed into national credit institutions. Under current law, commercial banks are legally incorporated as companies and a concession is not required. They now operate under a license[22] granted by the ministry of finance.

The new rules allow for foreign participation in banking, with up to a maximum of 30 percent of the capital. In addition, corporate rights of foreigners are now similar to those of national investors. These changes are designed to promote the capitalization of financial intermediaries, attract new technologies, and provide a wider network of links with international markets that will make Mexican banks ready for increased competition in the future.

There is a 5 percent maximum limit on the equity any individual may hold in a bank, with the possibility of increasing this limit up to 10 percent with the prior authorization of the ministry of finance. Regulations aim at ensuring that banks are controlled by Mexican shareholders, while promoting a sufficiently pluralistic and widespread participation in the capital of banks, thus avoiding an undesirable concentration in the decision-making process. Institutional investors are authorized to hold up to a 15 percent share as a means of providing indirect access to portfolio investments in a bank's equity to a large number of investors. In addition to the limits for bank equity ownership by nonfinancial corporations, the banking law limits the concentration of credit risk and stock investment by banks and ensures the separation of interests between banking and other activities. Neither may loans be made to the managers and partners of the banks.

The process of authorization for the establishment of banks and the regulation of their operations seeks to ensure that top executive officers and board members will be honest and technically qualified, and that banks will operate in accordance with sound banking practices. To guarantee the professional management of banks, the members of the board and the chief executive officer (CEO) must meet certain minimum requirements. The National Banking Commission must approve the designation of the members of the board, the statutory auditors, and the CEO, as well as other senior executives. Furthermore, the commission will be authorized to remove or suspend them under certain circumstances.

Finally, the new law permits foreign investment of up to 49 percent of the capital of insurance companies, bonding agencies, bonded warehouse companies, and leasing companies.

REFORMS TO THE STOCK MARKET ACT.   The Stock Market Act regulates the operation of the institution responsible for trading securities, and the reforms intend to contribute to increased marketability in the secondary market. To the already permitted activities of investment banking, brokerage, and management of mutual funds, the new act now provides for the role of the specialist who acts as both broker (for other brokers) and dealer on his own behalf in certain stocks he has been assigned. The specialist is responsible for maintaining a fair and orderly market in those stocks; he must sell when demand for these stocks is high and buy when it is low. In addition, the law was amended to allow foreign investment of up to 30 percent of the capital of brokerage firms, with a limit of 10 percent on individual shareholdings.

ACT REGULATING FINANCIAL GROUPS.   Several reforms in the "financial package" approved in December 1989 included provisions related to the integration of financial groups. During 1990, to promote the integration of such groups and the development of universal banking, the Act Regulating Financial Groups was issued, articles related to the financial groups were incorporated into the Credit Institutions Act, and the Stock Market Act was amended.

The law makes it advantageous for intermediaries to form financial groups. Their members may use similar names so that the public can recognize which organizations belong to the same group, and facilities and branch offices may be used to carry out the operations of any member of the group, thus sharing infrastructure costs.

Among the most relevant features of the reform is the possibility of establishing financial holding companies, which would become the hub for a universal banking system where a single financial group can provide all financial services. These groups will comprise a holding company and at least three of the following entities: deposit warehouses, financial leasing companies, brokerage firms, foreign exchange companies, and financial factoring agencies. As part of the new Credit Institutions Act, banks that do not belong to a financial group have the right to acquire a controlling interest in other financial institutions with the prior authorization of the ministry of finance. Brokerage firms and insurance or bonding companies may not be owned by a bank.

To protect the interests of those operating with members of financial groups, the holding company will own at least 51 percent of the shares and control the general assemblies and the board of directors of all the financial entities integrating the group. The composition of the holding company's capital stock, restrictions for shareholding, the shareholders' representation at meetings, the composition of the board of directors, the approval of its members and of the chief executive officer, as well as the removal and suspension of managers and executives, are subject to rules similar to those applicable to commercial banking institutions.

The holding company and each entity of the group will sign an agreement making the holding company fully responsible for the liabilities and losses of any of the financial entities of the group. However, each of the entities will not be held responsible for the holding company's losses nor for those of any other member of the group. This provision combines the main advantages of specialized financial intermediation with the benefits of a system of integrated financial services. The holding company cannot by itself assume any liability or perform operations that correspond to the intermediaries within the financial group.

d. Privatizing Commercial Banks
The legal reforms just described provided the basic framework with which to begin the divestiture of state-owned commercial banks and the orderly formation of financial groups. Whithin the broader context of the reform of the state, President Salinas sent to Congress an initiative to reform the constitution to allow for the privatization of banks, which was passed in mid-May 1990. In September a presidential decree was issued setting up a sales procedure which could guarantee transparency and at the same time be consistent with the objectives of a more efficient intermediation. Between 1991 and 1992, the divestiture process of all eighteen banks is to be completed. The details are discussed in chapter 4.

e. Financing the Government Deficit
Last but not least, the financial reform has also changed the way the budget deficit is financed. The increasing reliance on the money market, and therefore lower inflationary pressures, can been seen in the extent to which the Banco de México financed public sector borrowing requirements. The bottom line is that the outstanding balance of central bank credits to the nonfinancial public sector has come down, in real terms, at an average rate of 14.1 percent per year since 1982. This reassures the transition to non-inflationary deficit financing in market conditions, while granting increased independence for the central bank to conduct monetary policy (see table 2.4 and figure 2.6).

Table 2.4
Percentage changes on the balance of financing of the Banco de México to the nonfinancial public sector (real terms)

Nonfinancial	Public sector (% real terms)
1981	11.1
1982	27.8
1983	−12.6
1984	−18.2
1985	−10.6
1986	−11.6
1987	−45.4
1988	−2.2
1989[1]	40.1
1990	−11.3
1991	−35.2

Source: DGPH, Ministry of Finance.
1. This increase includes the credit for $1 billion given by the Banco de México to the federal government for guarantees to perform the exchange of UMS paper for Brady bonds (see chapter 3). If this is excluded, the increase would have been 25 percent.

1.2 The Social Dimension of the Financial Reform—A Case Study: Financing of Micro and Small Enterprises (1988–1991)

One frictional consequence of the structural change process in many Latin American countries has been the proliferation of an informal sector. When large inefficient public and private firms have been closed, or when the formal sector has not grown at the same rate, the informal sector, often taking the form of microenterprise, begins to absorb excess labor.

This phenomenon presents a challenge of extraordinary proportions for the economic and social policy of a country

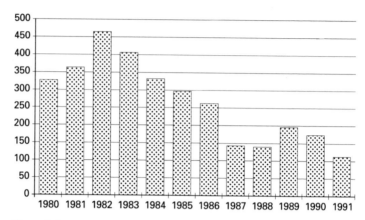

Figure 2.6
Outstanding credit from the Banco de México to the nonfinancial public sector (trillion pesos)
Source: DGPH, Ministry of Finance.

in which financial and labor markets are imperfect. At the same time, however, it creates a great opportunity to reshape industrial structure so that an authentic "grassroots capitalism" can flourish.

Having carefully looked at the experience of advanced countries such as Italy,[23] it can be concluded that a development strategy based on small enterprises makes sense, not only in terms of an equal distribution of income and opportunities, but also in terms of gaining a leading edge in increasingly competitive domestic and international markets.

In fact, an economic policy aimed at creating a balanced structure propitious for competition must recognize that there are phases in the production processes during which autonomous decisions in small productive units are clearly preferable to centralized decisions in a large firm. Such is the case of some high-quality clothing, furniture, and some other manufactures of low technological content. Nevertheless, there are activities such as marketing and commercialization in which obvious economies of scale keep small firms at a disadvantage. Consequently, it is desirable to have an industrial base that relies on small productive units in activities in which they are more efficient, and to promote forms of industrial organization that can exploit economies of scale where these may be present (e.g., in marketing, trade, etc.).

Over the past three years the apparatus of development financing has been completely overhauled. As a result, whereas in 1987 Nacional Financiera (the National Industrial Development Bank) allocated 94 percent of its total credit program to large inefficient parastatal enterprises, and the remaining 6 percent to small and medium-size enterprises, in 1991 it applied only 6 percent of its resources in credits to parastatal firms and 94 percent to loans to the private sector (about $15 billion) through commercial banks and nongovernmental organizations.

This new role for development banks has also implied a profound departure from previous thinking on development credits. Instead of being seen only as an instrument for alleviating poverty, development credits are now the subject of a much more competitive and businesslike approach. In practice, the new programs operate under the following principles.

• Development banks have to grant small producers access to credit, not subsidies. In terms of costs, it must be considered that small firms' only alternative is to borrow from credit sharks.

• Technical assistance and credit have to be seen as integral parts of the same package.

• Some programs require the participation of nongovern-mental organizations.

• To reduce costs and to help to develop a culture for formal credit in the community, it is advisable to take advantage of the infrastructure of commercial banks and other finan-cial intermediaries.

• The credit programs have to back all kinds of activities, from industry to commerce, agriculture, and services.

• As many firms as possible have to be reached without sacrificing the quality of the credits. In other words, the challenge is to launch massive and effective schemes.

Following these principles, Nacional Financiera (NAFIN), operating entirely as a "second-tier bank," has set up a two-level program designed to work as a "graduation process," starting with small firms without access to the commercial bank system and ending with firms ready to participate in the market economy.

Stage 1: Financing Programs for Micro Enterprises

This part of the program is designed to respond to the needs of *very small firms,* most generally family-based, with five or fewer employees, who in most cases are not registered in the Social Security system. These enterprises most com-monly do not pay either direct or indirect taxes, do not have an accounting method, and do not have access to commer-cial bank credit.

  Helping these kinds of firms can be extremely costly and very risky, because credits are usually very small (between U.S.$50 and U.S.$10,000), maturities very short (in most cases less than a year), and monitoring can be complicated, since many enterprises have, in principle, no accounting system.

As a result, for NAFIN the right strategy to reach this segment of the market was not to look for commercial banks to carry out the allocation of credits (not only because of the high monitoring costs involved, but also because commercial banks lack the structure to give technical support), but rather to rely on local nongovernmental organizations (NGOs), set up by larger entrepreneurs of a given community. These NGOs would use money from private sector contributions to provide the required training services and channel and administer credit resources coming from NAFIN. In addition, all thirty-one states of the Mexican federation have set up funds that use local tax proceeds to cover technical expenses, and, following the same mechanics described above for NGOs, provide credits with NAFIN resources to small private entrepreneurs.

It is important to stress that all credits are given to small firms without subsidy, and penalties for default consist of no further access. In turn, firms can benefit from this mechanism for no more than three years, after which they either "graduate" or reconsider seriously whether to stay in business.

The range of issues covered by technical assistance is very wide, from the basic concepts of accounting, administration, and marketing to engineering help in the design of products and processes. The help is provided by the staff of the NGOs or through cooperation programs with local universities, which sends students in their last year of studies to meet their requirement of "community service."[24]

The credit conditions are basically as follows: Nacional Financiera provides the financial resources for credit to the NGO or state (local) fund, which in turn provides the credit to the small entrepreneurs at a rate previously agreed upon with NAFIN. This rate is expressed in terms of a market rate (treasury certificates or CETES) plus a spread (between 6 and 10 percentage points) intended to cover the cost of monitoring and part of the technical assistance[25] (see table 2.5.).

Stage 2: Financing Small Enterprises

Once a firm has successfully created its own credit history in the program for micro enterprises, or if it employs fewer than fifteen people and/or has sales of less than (approximately) one million dollars, the program recognizes the importance of making entrepreneurs go through commercial banks, even though under normal conditions the banks would still find it too costly to make direct loans to these

Table 2.5
Micro and small enterprise financing framework (Nacional Financiera)

Type of enterprise	Business profile	Program
Micro enterprise	Firms with 5 or fewer employees, and sales of U.S. $100,000 a year or less in the industrial and commercial and services sector.	Credit and technical assistance through nongovernmental organizations and state (local) trust funds.
Small enterprises	Firms with more than 5 and fewer than 15 employees, and/or sales of U.S. $100,000 to U.S. $1,000,000 a year.	• Small business credit card. • Automatic discount in less than 24 hours. • Credit agreements through larger commercial enterprises. • Organization of guaranteed funds. • Use of already established financial intermediaries.

entrepreneurs with their own funds. For that reason, in this second stage NAFIN puts up the money and the banks do the work of administering the loan and carry its risk. In this way, within twenty-four hours, NAFIN discounts all commercial bank loans to small enterprises enrolled in the "small-business credit card" program. This is how it works: using a "point method" of credit rating, set jointly by NAFIN and the credit institution, the commercial bank decides if the applicant can enter the program (one week maximum). The credit limit goes from U.S.$10,000 to U.S.$250,000, and financing covers both working and fixed capital. The entrepreneur receives a plastic card that looks exactly like a bank credit card. However, this is not a credit card, but an identification card. He must show this credit card at the bank window any time he requires financing.

Upon presentation (and deposit) of invoices and/or orders, the entrepreneur will receive the requested amount within twenty-four hours. This means that there is no need to go through a lot of red tape every time he or she looks for funding. The cost of credit for the entrepreneur may vary, but it is typically CETES plus 600 basis points. The commercial bank assumes all risks and manages the loan. Its funding cost is the current CETES rates.

Initially, the financing of small enterprises involves commercial banks, but in the past few months the operation has been extended to include other kinds of intermediaries such as credit unions, factoring companies, and leasing companies. It is also worth noting that although the "credit card" idea works well as a "marketing" device, it is not indispensable as long as the criteria of automatic rating and expeditious credit are met. Once firms grow in terms of sales and employment and acquire business experience, they "graduate" once again and become eligible for direct commercial bank loans provided on purely market conditions.

In parallel credit is being used to support some forms of association organization among entrepreneurs, not only to open new ways of financing but to help exploit some of the economies of scale mentioned earlier. For example, trying to take advantage of economies of scale in credit operations, NAFIN has encouraged small entrepreneurs in the same field of activity to set up guarantee funds. In this way affiliated firms can have access to NAFIN credits through commercial banks at a favorable rate, or directly from NAFIN through specially designed trust funds. NAFIN also helps small business take advantage of economies of scale in marketing by financing small enterprises through super-market chains. The supermarkets can also function as trading companies for small business.

Although it is still too early to conclude that the Mexican experience has been an absolute success, it already shows some encouraging qualitative and quantitative results as the program gains momentum. For instance, whereas two years ago NAFIN gave credit and technical assistance to less than 40 new small enterprises a day, now it is supplying more than 250, all with the enthusiastic participation of commercial banks and other intermediaries who try to use this opportunity to gain new clients in the retail market. At the same time, the loans are performing with a repayment rate of 99.5 percent. On the quality side, there are hundreds of success stories of small entrepreneurs who, having started many times with the poverty lending programs of NGOs several years ago, have joined the NAFIN schemes and are planning to or now actually exporting their products to the United States (see table 2.6).

Table 2.6
The micro and small businesses program of NAFIN (1991)

Financing to micro and small firms (flow)	$2.4 billion during 1991
Number of firms benefited	74,000 (1989–1991)
	41,000 (only in 1991)
	39 a day in 1989
	250 a day in December 1991
"Small business" credit cards distributed	2,000 cards distributed by December 1990
	50,000 distributed by December 1991
Programs through other intermediaries	117 credit unions
	22 leasing companies
	4 factoring companies
	32 state development funds
	2 nationwide NGOs, with more than 50 chapters in all

1.3 Ten Thoughts on The Macroeconomics of Financial Reform

In addition to what the theory suggests should be the characteristics of financial reform, the fact that there have been cases in which financial liberalization has proved disastrous for stabilization goals, and also circumstances in which it has strengthened the other elements of the economic program, leads one to think that sequencing and speed play as crucial a role as the decisions of liberalization and deregulation themselves.

In spite of this, the case of Mexico can cast some light on the importance of financial factors in economic development. For that reason, I would like to conclude this section by listing what I think have been the ten most important lessons we have learned throughout our recent experience of financial liberalization.

1. *Before proceeding into financial liberalization, substantial progress must also be made in the stabilization of the economy, especially regarding the adjustment of public finances.* A financial liberalization program has to be seen as an integral part of a more comprehensive adjustment program. Lifting credit and interest rate controls in an economy with serious public finance disequilibria can make things much worse—pushing inflation even higher, instilling undesirable instability in the market, damaging confidence, and perhaps also aggravating the public finance disequilibrium.

2. *Financial liberalization has to go beyond the mere freeing of interest rates and the elimination of quantitative controls on credit.* The use of interest rate and quantitative controls on credit makes sense when financial markets are not capable of supporting intertemporal, intersectoral, and intergenerational transfers efficiently. In fact, the Mexican experience of the 1950s and 1960s showed us that financial repression, when combined with fiscal discipline, can help growth at the early stages of industrialization.

Lifting credit controls has to simultaneously address the issue of missing financial markets. For this reason a financial liberalization program should also look for the creation of new financial instruments, the updating of financial regulation to promote competition and facilitate supervision, a better linkage with international markets, and the promotion of technological development to improve the quality and speed of information.

3. *Timing and sequencing are important.* During the process of macroeconomic adjustment—especially in the case of small open economies where financial assets are internationally mobile—it is indispensible to have an effective non-

inflationary way to finance public sector borrowing needs, while stopping capital flight. Therefore it is extremely helpful to count from the early phases of adjustment with flexible-rate government instruments, which apart from their financing role can also help to develop a money market for both publicly and privately issued instruments that can offer attractive yields to the public. However, quantitative controls will have to wait longer before being removed. In fact, the experience of Mexico suggests that it is necessary to have achieved a small budget deficit and to have a money market that works reasonably well before completing the liberalization process.

4. *Don't experiment with the financial system.* It is always preferable to proceed prudently, granting the government enough instruments to intervene. Losing control can be as bad as or worse than having an overregulated system. The financial system, unlike the others sectors in the economy, is based on the trust and confidence of the public, and betraying them can have enormous costs in terms of the overall viability of the economy.

During the first stages of liberalization it is best to provide the regulation with some "cushions" to ensure the financial health of the intermediaries. For example, the system of precautionary reserves imposed on commercial banks is very conservative. On average, the precautionary reserves to total portfolio ratio in Mexico is more than twice the European average.

5. *Greater financial liberalization and innovation must be accompained by effective mechanisms of supervision.* Parallel to deregulation and the lifting of controls is the responsibility of the authorities to reinforce strict respect for the laws by clearly determining the roles of banking, insurance, securities, and other similar commissions.

6. The banking system has to be financially sound at the time of liberalization. If banks have financial problems when the authorities lift all restraints on their lending and borrowing rates, financial liberalization could lead them to an even weaker situation in terms of profitability and portfolio strength as they strive to increase their market share.

7. Financial intermediaries must be kept separate from their industrial and commercial clients. We have found that it is not desirable to have merchant banks and investment banks participating as permanent shareholders in commercial and industrial firms. This separation has the advantage of avoiding conflicts of interest and entry barriers created by using credit rationing to prevent competition in the nonfinancial sectors. However, this does not mean that financial intermediaries should abandon their roles as catalysts for new businesses and investment by participating temporarily as small shareholders in a company.

8. Before opening up the financial sector to international competition, it is advisable to give national institutions time to get used to conditions of increased internal competition. Financial liberalization will require additional investment on the part of the intermediaries to update their systems, buy new equipment, etc. If they are forced to face external competition at the same time, there is a risk that the financial system could be seriously displaced.

9. Once the liberalization process is completed, the next step is to move in the direction of universal banking. Financial groups can be developed to take advantage of economies of scale and information in financial markets. Also, they facilitate the creation of new instruments. As with the other elements of financial reform , this new stage has to be accompanied by close supervision to guarantee clarity and give greater confidence to the public. There has to be no doubt, however, that eventually this sector will be opened to international competition.

10. *It is essential to bear in mind that the reform of financial institutions can and must have a strong social impact.* The modernization of the development banking institutions, aside from supporting the correction of public finances and the elimination of price distortions, can have a lasting social and economic impact. More transparent and agile development banks are among the most useful elements of a policy geared toward offering everybody an opportunity to participate in the process of economic development.

2 Fiscal Reform

2.1 Background

The Mexican tax system has evolved substantially during the last forty years, having played very different roles during the various stages of the process of the country's development. For almost two decades after the Mexican Revolution, the tax system still contained, as it did during most of the second half of the nineteenth century, a large number of specialized levies on industrial production, the exploitation of natural resources (oil and mining industries), and international trade. This structure was not the result of any fiscal strategy for economic development, but rather a response to the need to get tax revenues from sources that were less expensive to collect from and to audit.

It was not until the mid-1950s that the authorities began to pay serious attention to the distributional and structural effects of tax distortions. Between 1955 and 1972, the authorities of the ministry of finance sent Congress a series of five major tax reform initiatives[26] aimed at building a basic framework consistent with the objectives of industrialization of that time. This "first tranche" in the tax reform of the last forty years included the substitution of a large number of production and sales taxes for a single and easier to administer turnover tax, the creation of a national registry of taxpayers, and an entirely new income tax approach that came to replace what was known as a "cedular system." Under the cedular system, different taxes were charged to individuals and corporations, depending on the source of income. This was replaced by a regime where taxes would be calculated on their "net *global* income," which means that the same tax rate would be applicable, irrespective of the source of income. The new income tax rules also included special regimes for agriculture, forestry, fishing, mining, transportation, and small enterprises, where each firm would pay a fixed amount irrespective of its performance, arbitrarily calculated by an employee of the revenue office. In practice, these special regimes translated into an almost complete tax exemption to those sectors.

The second round of reforms took place between 1978 and 1981,[27] partly in response to the adverse distributional effects of inflation through the tax system,[28] and in part with the intention of reducing the distortions implied by the "cascading" effect of the turnover tax. Seen from a long-term perspective, this "second tranche" of reforms was less "revolutionary" than the first , and in a sense it was more of an attempt to adapt the existing regulation to a new inflationary environment. In consequence, most of the essential issues of a tax system, such as the size and the distribution of the burden among income groups and sectors, were not addressed. Therefore, its bias in favor of "high priority sectors" and against labor income remained basically untouched (see tables 2.7 and 2.8).

Table 2.7
Main features of previous tax reforms

First series of reforms (1955–1972)	Administrative changes	• Setting up of the National Registry of Taxpayers. • Mechanization and computerization of information.
	Income tax	• Elimination of the system of "cellular" income taxes, which meant different tax rates depending on the source of income. • Setting up of a general regime for individuals and another for enterprises. Tax is applied on each regime irrespective of the source of income (tax on *global net income*). • For individuals, the minimum wage became deductible. • Introduction of rules allowing for accelerated depreciation. • Creation of "special regimes" known as *special tax bases* for small enterprises and the agricultural, livestock, and fishing sectors, for which tax is computed on the basis of a reference "global revenue" calculated by an official of the revenue office.
	Sales tax	A large number of taxes are substituted by a turnover tax that taxes every sale, including interfirm sales.
Second series of reforms (1978–1981)	Income tax	• Revision of the tax schedule for personal income tax to correct for the effects of inflation and some of the regressive bias from the previous reform. • Revision to the capital gains tax, acknowledging its nonrecurrent character and taxing only its impact on permanent income. Also the price cost and the reinvestments on assets are adjusted for general price increases.
	Sales tax	Introduction of VAT and the elimination of the turnover tax, 400 municipal and state taxes, and 30 federal excise taxes.

Source: Prepared with information from Estadísticas Históricas de México, INEGI, and DGPI, Ministry of Finance.

Table 2.8
Tax structure, 1925–1990
(revenues of each tax/total tax revenues of federal government, %)

	1925–1940	1941–1950	1951–1960	1961–1970	1971–1980	1981–1990
Tax on natural resources	7.61	4.72	2.59	2.58	1.97	2.85
Industry tax	26.22	14.06	—	—	—	—
Special tax on production	—	—	16.85	18.56	17.66	16.11
Import and export tax	35.94	27.22	30.30	18.47	15.42	23.85
Income tax	12.05	21.04	35.81	42.24	43.03	33.76
Payroll tax	—	—		1.93	0.98	0.77
Stamp tax	9.73	1.15	2.06	0.16	—	—
Commerce tax	2.11	9.67	9.60	—	—	—
Turnover tax	—	—	—	13.33	18.66	—
Value-added tax	—	—	—	—	—	21.65
Lottery tax	—	—	1.20	0.11	0.36	—
Immigration tax	—	—	0.27	0.27	0.06	—
Other taxes	6.34	22.14	1.31	2.35	1.86	1.01

2.2 The 1989–1991 Fiscal Reform

By the end of the 1980s, the capacity of the Mexican tax system to support a permanent program of social and infrastructure spending, as well as to correct the problems of income inequality, was seriously threatened by generalized evasion. The system was also plagued by a tax credit scheme conceived for a different industrialization strategy in effect twenty-five years before, an unfair personal income tax schedule that failed to keep up with inflation, and a corporate tax setting with rates significantly higher than those of our main trading partners.

As in the reforms of the 1950s and 1960s, once again it was necessary to update the tax system, not merely to adapt to changes in exogenous circumstances and policy making, but to respond adequately to the new development objectives of Mexico. Modernization had to take in everything from administrative procedures to a thorough revision of the structure of direct and indirect taxes. This time the new development strategy called for a set of rules compatible with an economy open to international competition and a more active private sector role in the industrialization of Mexico.

The tax structure in effect prior to 1989 placed the tax burden on individuals and a few sectors of the economy that had to pay very high rates in comparision with international standards. There were also privileged sectors that enjoyed tax-free status, without social or economic justification in an economy based on competition, dynamic investment, and rapid productivity growth. These weaknesses and inequities were addressed in the legislative initiatives passed by Congress between 1989 and 1991.

a. Income Tax Reform

The aim of the income tax reform was to significantly reduce the tax rates on corporations as well as on individual taxpayers to levels similar to those of our main trading partners. For overall tax revenues to at least maintain their level as a fraction of GDP, the tax base also had to be expanded. As a result, between 1989 and 1991 the corporate tax rate was brought down from 42 percent to 35 percent percent, while the maximum tax rate paid by individuals came down from 50 percent to 35 percent. Simultaneously, the personal income tax schedule was indexed to the consumer price index, and the corporate tax base was fully adjusted for inflation (see figure 2.7 and table 2.9).

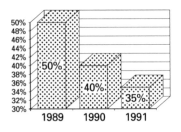

Figure 2.7A
A personal tax rate

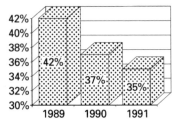

Figure 2.7B
Corporate income tax rate

In parallel with these reductions in rates, it was decided to introduce a tax of 2 percent on the total assets of those subject to the corporate income tax (except financial institutions) . This tax puts a floor on revenues, but the most profitable firms are not affected because the new tax can be fully credited against income tax. Coincident to the reduction in rates, the special tax regimes applicable to agriculture, fishery, forestry, livestock raising, truck and bus transportation, banks, and the book and newspaper industry left them either exempt or with very small contributions to general tax revenues. These special tax bases were elim-

Table 2.9
Comparison of income tax structure

	Mexico	United States	Canada
Average (federal, local, and state) corporate income tax rate (%)	35	38.3	43.3
Indexation of tax rates (%)	YES	NO	NO
Maximum rate of deduction for capital investment during the first year (%)	91	33.3	35

Source: DGPI, Ministry of Finance.

inated, subjecting these sectors to the standard regime applicable to the rest of the economy, or to a "consumption tax" based on the cash flow of the firm. Today agriculture, fishery, and livestock are also eligible for a 50 percent tax rate reduction, but are now obligated to keep records on all cash transactions.

For small enterprises, the special tax regime was replaced by a "simplified system." Although the new system still acknowledges the managerial limitations of such firms, it abandons the previous paternalistic approach, looking this time to introduce the incentives and conditions that will gradually incorporate small firms into a competitive economy. For instance, all small businesses selling U.S.$200,000 a year or less are obliged to register and set up a simple accounting system based on a cash flow book; instead of the tax being a fixed amount set at the discretion of some treasury employee, it is now calculated on the base of the "net withdrawals" of the firm. This change helps make these productive units go from self-consumption entities to competitive enterprises in a profit-oriented culture. The new tax system forces small business to learn to elaborate basic financial information, which not only helps them to meet their fiscal obligations, but also to evaluate themselves through time and against their competitors.

It is important to say that, in contrast to the tax legislation applicable to those firms in the "regular regime," the system for small firms contemplates much simpler rules for computing depreciation and does not include the obligation either to pay the tax on total assets or to keep a record of all expenses. As a matter of fact, for firms with sales below U.S.$100,000 a year, there are special allowances for blind deductions on wages, and commercial firms selling directly to the public are exempt from paying value-added tax (VAT).

b. Tax Administration Reform

To guarantee that the reductions in tax rates achieve their objective of a fairer distribution of the tax burden, without jeopardizing the level of tax revenues, it is indispensable to implement strong measures to strengthen tax collection. To that end, during the past three years the tax administration has been partially privatized as commercial banks collect all taxes. Customs warehouses will soon be totally operated by private sector firms, where all information collection, tax determination, and paperwork is performed by private customs agents whose number has increased by 80 percent because of liberalized entry rules.

As of today, 10 percent of taxpayers are subject to a random audit; 5 percent is carried out by the federal government and 5 percent by local authorities. As the process gradually reaches everybody, making it possible to construct a reliable data base, the percentage of audits will gradually decline.

In addition to the administrative changes, there have been important initiatives in the areas of auditing, prosecution, and enforcement to limit evasion. In this way, all firms with assets above U.S. $3.3 million or sales above U.S. $1.7 million per year, or that employ more than 150 people, have to undergo a yearly fiscal audit performed by an independent certified public accountant. Prosecution of fraudulent cases has been stepped up. Whereas between 1929 and 1988 there were only 2 criminal indictments for fiscal evasion, between 1989 and 1991 there were more than 200 resolutory sentences, all of them implying imprisonment.

c. Reduction of the General VAT Rate

The improvements made in tax collection and the administration of more progressive taxes have also opened the way for a rate reduction of the less progressive taxes. In this way the general VAT rate has been lowered from 20 and 15 percent to 10 percent in the context of the PECE negotiations, starting in November 1991. In addition Congress passed a reform that replaced the 6 percent, 15 percent, and 20 percent VAT rates applicable in the border regions of the country with a single 10 percent rate. This reform has been in effect since January 1, 1992.

d. Special Tax Scheme for Capital Repatriation
Although the economy had made important progress in terms of reducing inflation and enhancing growth potential, it was realized that capital repatriation had been precluded by the fact that people were afraid to return their money, because a large financial operation could easily be tracked by the revenue office, leading to audits of all those wanting to invest in the country. For this reason it was necessary to look for a mechanism that, while making people meet their fiscal obligation, could also grant them anonymity.

The scheme, under which nearly $10 billion has been already repatriated, works as follows: whoever wants to return money does not have to declare the operation, but anonymously buys "fiscal stamps" for 1 percent of the amount. Only if audited under normal procedures will the investor show the stamps to the inland revenue officer. Otherwise, the tax authorities will not be interested in whose money is entering the country.

e. Deductions and Exemptions
The third element of the reform consisted of a closer examination of the economic rationale of all exemptions and deductions of previous laws and the elimination of those

that were not fully justified. For instance, deductions related to meals and automobiles for executives are now more carefully qualified to make sure that they are linked to the operation of the enterprise and are not simply used as a way to get around tax obligations.

Finally, the scheme of investment tax credits in the form of deductions via accelerated depreciation was trimmed to include only those projects carried out outside the three main metropolitan areas of Mexico City, Guadalajara, and Monterrey (see table 2.10).

f. Results

Even with the reductions in rates, tax revenues have increased faster than the expansion of total production. Between 1989 and 1991, real nonoil tax revenues increased 29.5 percent, or 1.50 percent of GDP. Of that increase, 60 percent is explained by higher income tax revenues from a base that expanded from 1,920,000 to 2,904,000 taxpayers. The rest has come from an average real rate of growth in excess of 12 percent per year in VAT revenues and foreign trade taxes. This additional effort is then the result of a more equitable participation of all Mexicans, in a way that is fully consistent with the idea of moving forward in terms of efficiency and competitiveness, but that at the same time

Table 2.10
Scheme of accelerated depreciation outside large metropolitan areas

Years of depreciation	Deduction during the first year (%)
3	91
10	77
33	48

Source: DGPI, Ministry of Finance.

addresses the basic principles of a democracy in which there cannot be any justification for granting special privileges to any group (see table 2.11).

2.3 Ten Ideas about Fiscal Reforms

Long before the discovery of the Laffer curve, fiscal reforms were haunted by paradoxes that tend to over- and underestimate their effects on resource allocation, income distribution, and fiscal revenues. In reality, however, the economic and social effectiveness of a fiscal reform has to do as much with the elements that economic theory points out as important as with the political economy aspects of its implementation. For example, an adequate level of non-distortionary taxes depends not only on the performance of credit markets and the dynamics of population growth, as would be suggested by the life-cycle and permanent-income theories, but on the fact that markets are not perfect and economic reality is complex, which implies that issues regarding tax evasion, administrative simplification, and the handling of information also have to be included.

Analyzing in some detail the everyday experience of Mexican tax reform, one could find that in addition to the effects expected from what the theory says on grounds of efficiency, it has provided helpful and practical priciples to be followed in the future operation and updating of fiscal institutions and instruments. For example, it can be said that:

1. *Excessive tax rates legitimize tax fraud and evasion and weaken enforcement efforts.* The policy of reducing tax rates and the measures aimed at enforcing the law are part of the same package. Compliance can only be sought on rules that are feasible. Apart from questionable supply-side arguments, the reduction in rates can have important effects on total

Table 2.11
Tax revenues as a fraction of GDP

Country	Total tax revenues (% of GDP)	Country	Personal income tax (%)	Country	Corporate income tax (%)
Denmark	34.9	Venezuela	8.8	Ireland	14.4
Ireland	34.0	Chile	5.6	Belgium	13.0
Belgium	27.2	Ecuador	5.3	Denmark	12.4
Holland	25.9	Japan	4.7	Italy	10.9
U.K.	25.9	U.K.	4.0	U.K.	9.9
Italy	24.9	Holland	3.8	Holland	9.9
France	20.5	Belgium	2.8	Canada	8.1
Chile	19.8	United States	2.8	United States	7.0
Venezuela	17.2	Mexico (1988)	2.1	Japan	4.9
Canada	14.8	Mexico (1989)	2.3	France	4.8
United States	14.1	Mexico (1990)	2.2	Germany	4.0
Japan	13.4	Mexico (1991)	2.1	Mexico (1988)	2.5
Mexico (1988)	11.5	France	2.5	Mexico (1989)	2.7
Mexico (1989)	12.0	Italy	2.4	Mexico (1990)	2.9
Mexico (1990)	11.8	Denmark	2.1	Mexico (1991)	3.1
Mexico (1991)	12.0	Canada	2.0	Colombia	1.7
Germany	11.6	Colombia	1.8	Ecuador	1.5
Colombia	10.3	Ireland	1.6	Chile	1.0
Brazil	9.3	Brazil	1.4	Venezuela	0.8
Argentina	6.7	Germany	1.0	Brazil	0.4

Source: DGPI, Ministry of Finance.

revenues simply because people can now afford to run their businesses within the law.

2. *Foreign trade taxes and internal taxes are much better managed if they depend on a single authority.* Concentrating the administrative responsibility of tax collection in a single authority facilitates enormously the revenue-raising process, because it is possible to find economies of scale and because it makes it easier to cross-check information and therefore enforce compliance.

3. *Inexpensive, and many times cost-saving, administrative changes can have first-order effects on tax revenues.* An effective fiscal reform does not only mean a set of very complex changes of the legislative processes and accounting practices, which require of a profound knowledge of the economy. It also requires some practical thinking and common sense. One example of this is the simplification of VAT collection in Mexico, which simply by changing from 32 separate entities (one per state) to centralized management and decentralized supervision has generated an immediate revenue response.

4. *An up-to-date data base is fundamental.* Any improvement in the conceptual and legal tax reforms is bound to be fruitless without a reliable and easily accessible data base. For this reason the authorities have to make a special effort in the automatization areas of data processing and data banks, so that they can be used productively by all areas of the revenue office to detect problems, facilitate enforcement, and plan further improvements.

5. *Fair enforcement of penal punishments has had an important effect on compliance.* A fair tax system has to rest on the principle that a share of the tax burden is borne by all members of society, based on their capacity to pay and not on their ability to elude obligations. An effective enforce-

ment of the law is not simply a device to increase revenues; most of all it is a means of assuring social equality.

6. *On the other hand, strict enforcement has had no negative effect on the investor's confidence nor on capital repatriation.* Sometimes it is feared that although tax enforcement can benefit revenues in the short run, it will end up hurting them in the long term to the extent that investors could feel harassed by the obligation to pay more. However, reality shows that a stable macroeconomic environment based on healthy public finances is an even stronger magnet for new businesses. Therefore, compliance based on an equal and fair treatment to all taxpayers provides them with an even basis for competition and offers the business community a stable framework around which to plan and to invest for the future.

7. *Special tax regimes are not worth the distortions they cause.* In practice special tax regimes, such as priviliged treatment enjoyed by border zones regarding value-added tax, have only contributed to problems of control while providing little gains, if any, in terms of regional economic development.

8. *Tax reforms must not only revise rates or the definition of the base; they also have to improve the wording of the law.* The conceptual virtues of any optimal tax design can be totally lost in the phrasing. For example, vague definitions of categories such as fringe benefits create veritable fiscal monsters after a few years, creating incentives to convert wages into all sorts of material income and causing losses in revenue and gross inequities.

9. *Tax reforms can benefit from international cooperation.* Agreements to exchange information are the most practical and effective way to use international cooperation to support

fiscal reform. In practice they greatly reinforce the fiscal capability of governments.

10. A tax reform is not only a matter of economic efficiency, but a commitment to social justice. It would be a major mistake to look at the tax system only from the perspective of what it can offer in terms of macro stability and micro efficiency. In fact, it also has to play an important role in social policy. An effective reform has to address the need to apply resources to the most pressing needs of the poor, but it also has to create the incentives and provide equal opportunities for everybody to participate in the formal economy, to produce, compete, and achieve a better standard of living.

3 The New Social Spending Strategy: The National Solidarity Program

The whole process of the state reform, carried out through fiscal reform, privatization of public enterprises, financial reform, and debt renegotiation, has had the single-minded objective of strengthening the capacity of the government to respond to its basic mandate of guaranteeing macroeconomic stability, an environment propitious for the expansion of production and employment, the eradication of poverty, sufficient and opportune delivery of social services, and the provision of justice and public safety.

Looking at the issue of social justice through social spending from a medium-term perspective, its most noticeable feature is that during the 1970s, 32 percent of total programmable public sector spending went into parastatal sector enterprises. During the crisis period, much-needed resources were diverted to cover the losses of inefficient firms, bringing this figure to just below 28 percent in 1983 and 1984. Now, as the process of state reform proposed by

President Salinas advances, it has been possible to free resources from activities that do not adhere to the government's constitutional mandate. Instead, resources are now used with reponsibility to face the challenge of bringing better living conditions to those most affected during the years of crisis and adjustment (see table 2.12).

In his inaugural address President Salinas de Gortari recognized it as his duty—and that of the executive branch—to fight poverty, not only by spending more on social infrastructure with the resources from the privatization of public enterprises and the rationalization of spending in other areas of government, but by applying those resources more effectively.

The National Solidarity Program is part of the new approach to social spending to address the issue of extreme poverty. Starting in December 1988, the program has disbursed an average of U.S.$1 billion a year, which in spite of its modest size compared to GDP (.4 percent), has already achieved remarkable results, mainly because it has actively involved large and diverse sectors of the population.

The program is based on four main principles. The first respects the will, initiatives, and kinds of social organizations of local participants. The second is participation, meaning that the decisions are not taken unilaterally by the government but in accordance with the communities it wishes to benefit. The third is co-responsibility, which implies that each project is based on a covenant that establishes the share of the costs and responsibilities to be shouldered by each party (government and community). Finally, the fourth principle is clarity, meaning that every participant will be fully informed and able to respond fast to whatever happens without bureaucratic interference.

Table 2.12
Social spending of the federal government

Year	% of GDP	% of programmable spending of the public sector
1971	5.3	31.7
1972	6.3	33.7
1973	6.3	30.1
1974	6.7	30.6
1975	7.3	27.8
1976	8.1	32.9
1977	7.8	33.7
1978	7.9	32.7
1979	8.4	33.4
1980	8.1	31.0
1981	9.2	31.2
1982	9.1	33.8
1983	6.7	28.0
1984	6.7	27.6
1985	5.0	22.6
1986	6.6	30.7
1987	6.2	30.6
1988	6.1	32.0
1989	6.2	35.5
1990	6.5	37.9
1991	7.6	43.7

Source: Cuenta Publica, SPP, several issues.
1. Social spending is defined as total outlays in education, health, and regional development.

In practice, the action programs of Solidarity begin with the creation of a Solidarity Committee in a given town or neighborhood, formed by the families of that community. This committee, according to its needs, puts forward a proposal and together with the authorities designs a scheme in which the raw materials for the project—such as the bricks, cement, and wood for refurbishing a school, or the cables and lampposts needed to electrify a town—are usually provided by the government, the engineering skills by university students, and the work force by the local people.

The projects conducted through Solidarity can be classified into three main groups. Social expenditure, which represents almost 55 percent of total Solidarity spending, implies the introduction of drinking water and sewerage to rural and marginal communities, electrification, the supply of basic foodstuff, the construction of rural medical facilities, and the conservation and reconstruction of school facilities. The second stream of projects is known as *Solidarity for Production*; using 30 percent of its resources, this program provides financial support to very small producers in economically depressed rural areas, which would not be eligible even for access to NAFIN microenterprise programs, to help them make the transition from subsistence agriculture to more productive activities while deepening their roots in the region. Finally, the third type of activity is known as Solidarity for Basic Support Infrastructure and Regional Development, which provides funds to enhance the municipal capacity to respond to social needs, and carries out road and local highway resurfacing projects (see table 2.13). Solidarity works because it links new elements in our complex society with long-standing traditional customs of participation.

Table 2.13
National Solidarity Program: The facts (1989–1991)

• More than 64,000 Solidarity Committees have been formed in low-income neighborhoods.

• These committees have carried out more than 150,000 projects.

• Six million people have been incorporated into health services in the facilities provided by the program.

• Eight million people got access to drinking water.

• Eleven million people in more than 10,000 communities now have electricity.

• Streets have been paved in 3,000 rural and urban communities.

• 14,000 kilometers of roads have been built, reconditioned, or improved, benefiting almost 2 million inhabitants.

• 1,400,000 children are receiving an education in the new school facilities refurbished by parents and teachers through the "Decent School" Program.

• Almost a quarter of a million children have been granted cash scholarships to enable them to complete their primary education without having to drop out due to their parents' lack of funds.

• The number of community dairies has more than doubled, and almost 7 million children have access to this basic foodstuff; 27 million people have access to basic commodity stores.

• The postal service has been extended to 4 million inhabitants in low-income neighborhoods and rural areas.

• 1,200,000 registered property deeds have been delivered to an equal number of families in low-income neighborhoods.

Source: Third State of the Nation Address, Presidency of the Republic.

4 Concluding Remarks

The fiscal and financial policies of a government cannot be seen exclusively as instruments with which to achieve macroeconomic stability and create a good environment for business. In fact, they are powerful tools with which to carry out an effective social policy. The examples of the fiscal reform of the last three years, the NAFIN microenterprises schemes, and the National Solidarity program are examples of ways in which macroeconomics and development are linked by the higher mission of a government before its people.

The reform of the state, under the leadership of President Salinas de Gortari, has introduced new ways to increase popular participation in civil society in the context of a fairer distribution of income and opportunities.

3   Structural Change of the External Sector

Macroeconomic and structural adjustment in Mexico has taken place in the context of a profound transformation of the world economy. In part as a result of the upsurge of protectionism and the energy shocks of the last fifteen years, and in part as a consequence of the dynamics of technological change and the worldwide pattern of industrialization, commerce has moved away from a collection of fragmented national markets weakly linked by trade flows to a much larger global market; firms do not have to be next to their "natural" national market to succeed, but can effectively separate geographically the design, production, financing, and distribution phases of their activity.

As a result of these changes, our own idea of national industries and national development policies has had to expand. The proliferation of joint ventures and foreign investment flows has blurred the once clear correspondence between the growth potential of national enterprises and opportunities to enhance economic welfare. Successful national policy is no longer based on the idea of overprotecting local markets and local producers, but rather on creating an economic environment that offers both domestic and foreign firms the right combination of regulation, infrastructure, skilled labor, and macroeconomic stability to produce efficiently and compete in the global market.

The process of integration with the world economy is very complex and generally implies establishing an ample set of policy measures, including deregulation, harmonization of legal, financial, and tax systems, and monetary integration. In spite of this complexity, experiences such as that of the European Community suggest that there is a sequence of decisions to be made—and consequently a place to start in the long road from autarky to a full participation in the international system. In general, this sequence begins with the removal of all obstacles to the free movement of goods and services and the establishment of a legal framework to facilitate the flows of foreign investment, as well as a flexible financial background to support currency stability and opportune trade financing.

From the viewpoint of Mexican development strategy, the opening up to trade and investment flows has meant a drastic change in the direction and emphasis of long-term industrial, commercial, and financial policies. In fact, between 1940 and 1982, Mexico's development scheme had two main characteristics regarding its relationships with the external sector. First, domestic industry was overly protected by conspicuous tariff and nontariff barriers, as well as very restrictive foreign investment rules. Second, the financial sector was so segmented that it induced self-financing of enterprises and external financing of the government deficit. As a result of these policies, Mexico's industrialization process had to progressively rely on government investment to keep up with the required expansion of employment and economic activity. The inefficient industrial base began to need more and more real exchange rate adjustments to keep up with foreign exchange needs, instead of facing external competition with higher productivity. At the same time, the financial stability of the country became increasingly threatened by capital flight responses to any internal or external sign of trouble.

The extent of the effects of these distortions on the economy could only be assessed during the worst months of the debt crisis of 1982. Then the viability of the economy was called into question by the threat of massive bankruptcies and layoffs, while inflation and stagnation dominated the future outlook.

This chapter reviews the experience of the Mexican external sector from the perspective of the long-term internationalization of its economy. Section 1 looks at the nature of the old mechanism of transmission behind the oil boom and debt crisis, and describes the process of debt renegotiation and the gradual restoration of access to international financial markets. Section 2 reviews the trade liberalization measures adopted since 1985, including the free trade agreements either already signed or under negotiation, and finally section 3 comments briefly on the reform of foreign investment rules and on other related areas of economic deregulation.

1 The External Debt Renegotiation

1.1 Background

The history of the Mexican debt crisis is very long. It starts with the default of the 1821 loans only three years after they were contracted, and continues with the suspension of payments and rescheduling exercises repeated half a dozen times during the rest of the nineteenth century, as the country was alternatively affected by internal wars, foreign invasions, and its own international business cycle.

The short period of solvency between 1890 and 1910 was once again interrupted, this time by the violent events of the Mexican Revolution, and the downturn was prolonged by the unfavorable external conditions of a world economy in recession. It was not until the signing of the Suárez-Lamont Agreement in 1942 that the country was able to enjoy continued access to international credit markets (see table 3.1).

During the 1950s and 1960s external financing, although present, did not play a significant role in the promotion of growth. On the public sector side, the years of the *desarrollo estabilizador* were characterized by very modest budget deficits that were covered by non-inflationary "forced" financing obtained from the reserve requirements imposed on commercial banks. Only a small fraction of the overall requirements came from official foreign sources.

On the other hand, investment in the private sector was essentially financed from its own savings. The reason for this is related to the way in which the industrialization strategy was originally set up. In practice, the mechanisms of industrial promotion behind the import-substitution and infant-industry policies allowed firms to generate rents, which in the absence of an efficient framework of intermediation were reinvested in the expansion of the same industries. The natural limits to this expansion were imposed by the size of the market and the meager incentives for technological change implicit in a business environment sheltered from internal and external competition.

This combination of fiscal discipline and private self-financing worked reasonably well for almost twenty years. By the beginning of the 1970s, however, it became apparent that the sources that supported the dynamics of private industry and employment expansion had to either face a

Table 3.1
Public external borrowing (1965–1991)

	Budget balance/GDP (%)	Net public external borrowing/GDP (%)[1]
1965	−0.8	−0.01
1966	−1.1	1.75
1967	−2.1	2.19
1968	−1.9	1.33
1969	−2.0	1.45
1970	−3.4	1.25
1971	−2.3	1.07
1972	−4.5	0.33
1973	−6.3	2.91
1974	−6.7	4.00
1975	−9.3	4.85
1976	−9.1	5.59
1977	−6.3	3.48
1978	−6.2	2.42
1979	−7.1	2.40
1980	−7.5	1.64
1981	−14.1	4.22
1982	−16.9	3.44
1983	−8.6	2.23
1984	−8.5	0.02
1985	−9.6	−0.01
1986	−15.9	0.27
1987	−16.0	2.03
1988	−12.4	−0.01
1989	−5.5	−0.21
1990	−4.0	0.78
1991	−1.5	−0.21

Source: Criteria for Economic Policy in 1992, Presidency of the Republic.
1. Banco de México, capital account of the public sector.

profound change in direction toward an export-driven strategy or be replaced by a public-sector-driven, foreign-debt-financed model of growth. At the time the authorities opted for the latter.

In the absence of any significant fiscal and/or financial reform, the permanent public spending expansion already under way by 1973 resulted in a substantial acceleration in the rhythm of foreign financing well above the average of the previous decades. For instance, in that year the flow of foreign debt reached $1.6 billion, compared with the average of $200 million a year during the 1960s.

Given the dynamics of events, it was not long before the country experienced a serious financial crisis. In 1976, the twenty-two-year era of fixed parity to the dollar ended, and for the first time the level of outstanding foreign public debt ($21 billion, as compared with $6.8 billion in 1972) and the size of the budget deficit (10 percent of GDP compared with 2.5 percent on average in the previous twenty years), raised serious doubts about Mexico's entire development policy.

The adjustment program, implemented in 1977 and backed by an IMF standby agreement, achieved the immediate goal of stabilizing the use of foreign financing. Unfortunately it failed to address the deeper questions about long-term growth and development perspectives.[1] In fact, less than two years after this first crisis those fundamental questions remain unanswered, and the whole adjustment program was abandoned. The emphasis on public expenditure to achieve high GDP growth became visible once again only a year after the López Portillo government took office, based on the grounds that the new oil wealth would finance Mexico's development in a non-inflationary way. Taking advantage of such wealth required the expansion of public investment. It was also said, however, that the government would use other policy instruments to strengthen the economy. Among these would be a reform of the financial sector, to make interest rates more flexible and responsive to market conditions, and a fiscal reform to include the introduction of a value-added tax. Whatever the arguments, the fact is that the internal and external imbalances accelerated rapidly, and external borrowing grew at an unsustainable pace. For instance, between 1980 and 1982 the stock of public foreign debt grew from 20.9 percent of GDP to 29.8 percent, whereas private indebtedness passed from 7.9 percent to a little more than 18 percent of GDP (see tables 3.2 and 3.3).

In sharp contrast with previous crises, the dynamics of economic collapse of the early 1980s revealed the Mexican economic structure to be much weaker than what had been anticipated six years before. This time, public borrowing was accompanied by heavy private borrowing in the international markets, coupled with an extremely rapid deteri-

Table 3.2
Evolution of total external debt (1976–1982)

		Stock of foreign debt ($U.S. millions)			Foreign debt/GDP	
Year	Public	Private	Commercial banks	Total	Public	Total
1976	20.8	4.9	1.6	27.3	24.9	32.6
1977	23.8	5.0	1.8	30.3	27.8	35.8
1978	26.4	5.2	2.0	33.6	25.7	32.7
1979	29.7	7.9	2.6	40.2	23.2	31.4
1980	33.8	11.8	5.1	50.7	20.9	31.3
1981	52.1	14.9	7.0	74.0	27.6	39.1
1982	58.1	18.0	8.0	84.1	29.8	43.1

Source: Solís and Zedillo (1985).

Table 3.3
Public sector finances

	Government spending/ GDP	Revenues/ GDP	PSBR/ GDP
1976	37.9	28.8	9.1
1977	29.9	23.6	6.3
1978	31.2	25.0	6.2
1979	32.6	25.5	7.1
1980	34.4	26.9	7.5
1981	40.9	26.8	14.1
1982	47.2	30.3	16.9

Source: DGPH. Ministry of Finance.

oration of expectations and massive capital flight. A study by Solís and Zedillo[2] suggested that excess borrowing during the 1979–1981 period was not simply the consequence of an intertemporal substitution of oil proceeds for present consumption, or a cushion to temporary terms of trade shocks. Rather "internal factors," such as an overheated economy and capital flight, would explain more than 80 percent of the story. What the exercise did was to compare observed borrowing with the flows of financing to be expected from the trends of each of the components of the balance of payments. For instance, excess imports attributed to too much public and/or private spending were classified as internal sources of overborrowing. The deterioration in terms of trade, reflected in a less than expected value of exports due to the decline in export prices, or higher spending as a result of higher interest rates, were labeled external shocks. Finally, the capital flight component was categorized as excess errors and omissions and private capital flows. The experience of these years, as summarized in figure 3.1, provides a very clear picture of how the lack of flexibility in the industrial sector, the corresponding use of fiscal disequilibria to maintain the growth rate of employment in the formal sector, and an incomplete and distorted financial sector can have serious effects on the dynamics of external borrowing and capital flight.[3]

1.2 The 1982 Debt Crisis

The chronology of the 1982 financial crisis begins with the sudden deterioration in the terms of trade by mid-1981, caused mainly by the reduction in the international price of oil and the increase in world interest rates, which triggered the acceleration of capital flight. After a devaluation in February of 1982 and the implementation of a rather mild economic adjustment program, the peso continued under heavy speculation. Although a new devaluation was

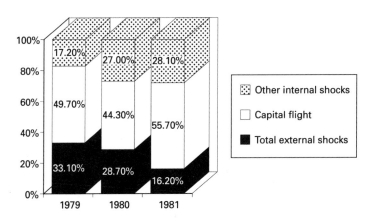

Figure 3.1
Causes of external overborrowing (1979–1981)
Source: Solís and Zedillo (1985).

avoided for several months, this was achieved only at the expense of exhausting foreign exchange reserves and using the last available credit lines. The end of the road was reached on August 20, when the ministry of finance asked Mexico's commercial bank creditors for a three-month moratorium on payments of principal as well as for the formation of a bank advisory committee to study and reach a negotiated solution. Between then and December, Mexico would accumulate an arrears of $8 billion in payments of principal of public sector debt, and the De la Madrid administration would assume power with the bleak prospect of another $14 billion coming due in the next three years (see table 3.4).

The 1982–1983 debt renegotiation had to address the immediate question of possible default without referring to the more fundamental problem of debt overhang, which would eventually imply negative net external transfers of the order of 6 percent of GDP in the following six years. The financing package resulting from the agreement with

Table 3.4
Balance of payments indicators ($U.S. millions)

	Current account	"Other" capital flows and errors and omissions (capital flight)	Change in reserves
1977	−1,596.4	−1,307.6	657.1
1978	−2,693.0	−210.4	434.1
1979	−4,870.5	−2,175.5	418.9
1980	−10,739.7	−3,470.1	1,018.5
1981	−16,052.1	−10,627.0	1,012.2
1982	−6,221.0	−10,466.7	−3,184.8

Source: Banco de México, Indicadores Económicos.

the advisory committee and the international financial institutions contained three main elements:

a. Rescheduling of all payments due between 23 August 1982 and 31 December 1984,[4] to be paid over a period of eight years, with a four-year grace period at a very high cost of LIBOR plus 1.875 or prime plus 1.75, at the choice of bank creditors.

b. Additional financing through an IMF standby agreement and the arrangement of a syndicated loan with more than 500 banks, amounting to $5 billion with a tenure of six years with three of grace and a cost of LIBOR plus 2.5 or prime plus 2.125, obviously at a penalty cost.

c. Restructuring of the private foreign debt. Because the government had decided not to assume the private external debt and that debtors would not receive any subsidy to settle their foreign obligations, it was decided to establish a mechanism to encourage the restructuring process. It would offer coverage for exchange rate risks on principal and interest payments that were rescheduled according to the guidelines issued by the financial authorities.[5] By the deadline in October 1983, private liabilities for almost $12 billion had been registered and covered by this mechanism.

The collapse of oil prices in 1986 and its macroeconomic impact, already mentioned in chapter 1, gave rise to new and very serious payments difficulties. Another renegotiation would have to be sought in spite of the extraordinary size of the adjustment program and the gradual but sustained process of real exchange rate depreciation initiated in mid-1985. In the end, the renegotiation of 1986 shared the same basic elements of the previous agreement: This time the "new money" component would be $14 billion, with the restructuring of outstanding debt with commercial banks and the Paris Club. The agreement with creditor banks of March

1987[6] rescheduled amortization payments on $43.7 billion of principal over twenty years, with a seven-year grace period. This figure included the entire medium-term commercial bank debt at the end of 1982 and the new $8.6 billion borrowed in 1983 and 1984. The prime rate was no longer used as the reference rate, and the spread over the base rate was reduced from a weighted average of 1.2 percentage points to 13/16 on the $43.7 billion, and from 1.5 percentage points to 13/16 on the $8.6 billion (see table 3.5).

Although these two renegotiations met the primary objective of allowing the country to keep servicing its debt, it was evident that the country's problem was not one of cash flow, but rather of debt overhang that imposed strict limits on its growth potential. It is important to stress that by 1986, this perception was not exclusively Mexico's; financial markets had already begun to acknowledge the per-

Table 3.5
Valuation of debt reduction and debt service reduction options (per dollar)

Assumptions[1]	
	Risk-free interest rate = 8.5%
	Mexico risk discount rate = 17%
	Spread paid over LIBOR = 13/16
Debt reduction bond (face value of 65 cents on each dollar of base debt).	PV of the zero-coupon bond = 5.6 cents
	PV of collateralized interest payments = 10.3 cents
	PV of noncollateralized interest payments = 25.7 cents
	Total = 41.6 cents
Debt service reduction bond (face value = 100, fixed rate of 6.25%).	PV of the zero-coupon bond = 8.6 cents
	PV of collateralized interest payments = 10.6

1. These assumptions reflect essentially the market conditions at the time at which the agreement was reached in principle.

manent nature of the crisis, as was evident from the building up of commercial bank reserves and the substantial discounts at which sovereign developing-country debt was traded in the secondary markets.

At that point, there were basically two options. The first was to postpone the decision to recognize the structural character of the debt overhang, and to push not only Mexico but the rest of the debtor countries into a prolonged recession very much like that of the 1930s.[7] The second was to look for a mechanism through which to distribute the losses incurred in the overlending process, according to each party's capacity to pay.

A careful conceptual revision of the way in which international lending takes place showed that some forms of debt forgiveness could actually be Pareto improving. Forcing the debtor country to continue to pay in full via a prolonged recession would only undermine incentives to implement correct economic reforms, because the only beneficiaries would be foreign creditors. Therefore some form of relief would actually increase the creditors' chances of recovering part of what was lent in the first place, to the extent that the arrangement gave the debtor enough room to resume growth.[8]

Prior to the 1989 renegotiation, the De la Madrid administration implemented two market-based debt reduction schemes that provided a valuable experience for the design of the 1990–1994 financing package. First, a debt/equity swap program in place from 1986 to mid-1988[9] helped make it understood that not all market-based schemes were desirable from the point of view of macroeconomic stability and efficiency.[10] For example, it was recognized that these kinds of swaps generated adverse fiscal effects, in that they meant a prepayment of debt, subsidy to investment, and additional monetary pressures through potential monetization.

To perform swap operations, the Mexican authorities needed pesos to pay for the debt to be exchanged. If these pesos came from the Banco de México, it was to be through more inflation and/or the loss of international reserves. If these pesos were obtained in the market through additional issues of internal public debt, the result would have been an increase in domestic interest rates and the crowding out of other investment projects. Another important impact had to do with the fiscal cost implied by the exchange of external debt (for which the authorities were paying international interest rates) for internal debt, whose cost was substantially higher. Last but not least, the need to ration these operations (or to move gradually, for that matter) for the sake of short-term macroeconomic stability introduced a serious distortion that inhibited foreign investment. Potential entrants interested in capturing the subsidy implicit in each operation postponed their investment projects, waiting for the next round.

The second program, launched on 29 December 1987 (two weeks after the beginning of the PSE), consisted of a ground-breaking proposal that commercial banks voluntarily exchange part of the existing debt for twenty-year bonds. The newly issued marketable bonds,[11] to be amortized in a single payment, offered a spread of 1⅝ percent over LIBOR and a nonmarketable U.S. Treasury zero-coupon bond with a thirty-year maturity as collateral. In the auction of debt for the new twenty-year bonds, Mexico accepted bids for $3.7 billion in foreign claims, at an average price of approximately 70 cents on the dollar of existing debt. The authorities invested $492 million in U.S. Treasury zero-coupon bonds as collateral. This second approach to market-based debt reduction operations proved to be a real watershed, although the volume traded was only marginal compared to the financial needs of the country. It became clear that it would take a very complex negotiation to perform an exchange operation of a larger magnitude. However, it was the direct precedent of similar proposals known as the Miyazawa Plan, the Mitterrand Plan, and eventually the Brady Plan, in which the industrialized countries of the world endorsed debt reduction (see figure 3.2).

1.3 From Debt Rescheduling to Debt Relief: The Renegotiation of 1989

Since the start of the debt crisis, both academics and policy makers warned that the problems of asymmetric information and policy inconsistency implicit in the way in which sovereign debt operations work would make any market-based solution extremely difficult.[12] For example, even

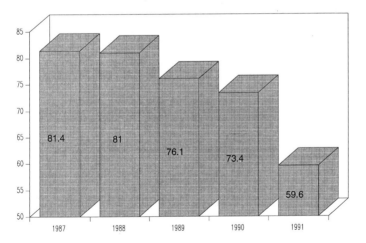

Figure 3.2
Economic external debt of the public sector (% of GDP)
Source: SAFI, Ministry of Finance.

though it had been accepted that debt reduction operations[13] could be Pareto improving (which means that when comparing the pre-exchange situation with the ultimate solution, everybody would prefer the second), the problem was how to get from the bad equilibrium to the good equilibrium, because each creditor bank would get a capital gain by simply waiting to see if the remaining banks were to participate in the buyback operation. This would mean that any voluntary exchange would necessarily face a free-rider type of externality, which would make it impossible for it to happen in the first place. This simple case of market failure gave rise to very concrete guidelines in the design of the renegotiation. First, the operation had to be big and comprehensive; that is, it had to include all renegotiable debt. Second, it required direct negotiation with the bank advisory committee, as well as the full cooperation of international financial institutions and G-7 governments, to get around the coordination and free-rider problems. Finally, to make it possible for all banks to participate fully, the financing package had to recognize the regulatory differences among countries, as well as the financial heterogeneity of the banks, by presenting them with a menu of value-equivalent alternatives instead of a single option.

In his inaugural speech on 1 December 1988, President Salinas de Gortari instructed the minister of finance to start the renegotiation of the external debt at once, according to the following four criteria:

a. Immediate reduction of the amount of outstanding debt;

b. Long-term reduction in the external debt burden defined in terms of the debt/GDP ratio;

c. Reduction in the net transfer of resources abroad;

d. A multiyear arrangement that would eliminate the uncertainty of recurrent renegotiations.

It was then decided that this process, which started immediately, would take place in two stages. The first stage included the arrangement of a financing package with international financial organizations and with the Paris Club with a double purpose; to reduce the levels of net transfers to these entities to zero by means of "fresh resources" contracted on a multiyear basis, and to count on the technical and political assistance of these institutions. The second stage would involve the negotiation of a large-scale debt reduction operation with commercial banks.

On 26 May 1989, an agreement was finally signed with the IMF.[14] Along the lines of the Brady Plan, the most important feature of this arrangement was that in addition to the resources it would provide over a number of years[15] to support the stabilization program, the institution acknowledged the need to carry out debt reduction operations and committed itself to set aside additional resources to be used as collateral in such operations. Thanks to the courageous and visionary proposals of Nicholas Brady, U.S. Secretary of the Treasury, the position adopted by the IMF signaled a profound change in the attitude of official institutions toward the debt problem and certainly set a precedent for other financial agents to emulate.

On May 30, Mexico reached an accord with the Paris Club to restructure short-term credits while obtaining new credit lines. The outcome was the rescheduling of principal payments of $2.6 billion over a ten-year grace period, which would mean relief of 100 percent of principal and interest between June of 1989 and March 1990, 100 percent of principal and 90 percent of interest until March 1991, and 100 percent of principal and 80 percent of interest until May 1992. Most important, the Paris Club would provide export credit guarantees for around $2 billion a year until 1992.

Finally, and only a few weeks later,[16] the World Bank followed through with an agreement to provide structural adjustment credits for $1.96 billion in 1989, and an average of $2 billion during the 1990–1992 period. It would also set aside resources for debt reduction operations that would eventually exceed those supplied by the IMF.

With the backing of this financing package and the track record of its own internal adjustment program carried out for more than six years, Mexico began negotiating with the more than 500 commercial banks represented by the bank advisory committee. A successful operation would make it possible to capture the relief implicit in the secondary market valuation of the external debt, given the available resources for guarantees.

Let me comment briefly on the considerations that influenced the design of the debt exchange options presented to the banks. The base debt—that is, the amount of commercial debt subject to the exchange operation—amounted to $48,231 million.[17] The price of the so-called UMS paper in the secondary market was then close to 42 cents for each dollar of nominal debt. This meant that if Mexico were to buy back all of its outstanding debt, it would have to pay $20.2 billion. The resources available from the IMF (U.S.$1.64 billion), the World Bank (U.S.$2.06 billion), the export-import bank of Japan (U.S.$2.05 billion), and the reserves of the Banco de México (U.S.$1.3 billion) totaled only $7 billion.

The proposal put forward by Mexico and the bank advisory committee to the participating banks consisted of a menu with the following three options:

a. Exchange at par value old (dollar-denominated or its equivalent in other currencies) debt for bonds with a 6.25 percent fixed interest rate (or its equivalent, depending on the currency), with semiannual interest payments and amortization in a single payment after thirty years. The bonds carry principal collateral of U.S. Treasury zero-coupon bonds, as well as a rolling interest guarantee of eighteen months on interest payments.

b. Exchange at a 35 percent discount old debts for a discount bond with interest rate of LIBOR plus 13/16 (or its equivalent in other currencies), with semiannual interest payments and amortization in a single payment at maturity in thirty years. Discount bonds would have the same guarantees on principal and interest as the par bonds.

c. Exchange old debts for new debt instruments with a fifteen-year maturity and a seven-year grace period, with an interest rate of LIBOR plus 13/16, together with a commitment to grant financing under the same terms during the period 1990–1992 for an amount equivalent to 25 percent of the debt allocated to this option through a combination of the following four instruments: purchase of new-money bonds, traditional medium-term bank credits, the relending program to the public sector, or the foreign trade financing program.

Looking carefully at the debt reduction and debt service reduction options, it can be claimed that both were buyback equivalent. This means that in each case the relief reduction would be the same as if the resources used to guarantee each option were used to buy Mexican debt directly in the market at going market prices at the time when the negotiation started.[18] As an example, one could take a debt reduction bond (option b) and prove that, given the conditions in the credit and secondary debt markets, it was worth 42 cents on the dollar at the date of exchange.

As shown in table 3.5, the value of this bond has three components. First, there is the zero-coupon bond, which is used to collateralize the principal and will be worth 100 cents per dollar in year thirty. The present value of this part is computed simply by discounting the bond at a risk-free market rate (for instance, the rate on thirty-year Treasury bonds). The second part corresponds to the first eighteen months of interest payments that were guaranteed by deposits at the U.S. Treasury Department. The present value of these flows is also discounted at the risk-free interest rate. Finally, regarding all remaining interest payments (and to the extent they were not insured against "Mexico risk"), they must be discounted at the internal rate of discount of the Mexican debt (UMS) as quoted on the secondary market (at that time the UMS had a yield to maturity of around 17 percent). Adding these three elements, the value of the Brady discount bond would be around 42 cents and the Brady par bond would be less than 46 cents on the dollar (see figures 3.3 and 3.4).

The final distribution chosen by the creditor banks was 47 percent of eligible debt to the par bonds, 41 percent to discount bonds, and 12 percent to the new money option. Discount bonds allocated to Mexican commercial banks represented 11.91 percent of total discount bonds and were not guaranteed due to the scarcity of resources (see figure 3.5).

The direct outcome of the package with commercial banks was a $7.19 billion reduction in principal and a decrease in net resource transfers of $U.S.4,071 million per year, on average, between 1990 and 1994, resulting from an annual savings in interest payments for $1,629 million, new money

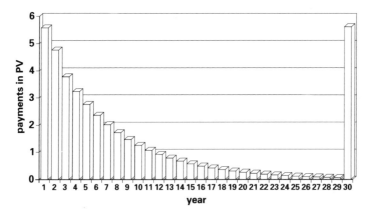

Figure 3.3
Present value of the flows of a Brady discount bonds (cents per dollar of face value)

amounting to $U.S.288 million, and the deferral of principal payments of $U.S.2,154 million due during that period (see figure 3.6).

Another direct effect of the renegotiation is that the agreement in principle with commercial banks in mid-1989 allowed Mexico to reenter voluntary international financial markets. The first issue since 1982 by a Mexican borrower, totally unrelated to any debt restructuring, took place in June 1989 when the Banco Nacional de Comercio Exterior[19] placed bonds for $U.S.100 million. Since then, at least $3.5 billion have been borrowed in the Euromarkets by Mexico's corporate and banking sectors, using a variety of instruments such as Eurobonds, EuroNotes, Floating Rate Notes, Floating Rate Certificates of Deposit, Euro CDs, Convertibles,[20] and Collateralized Receivable Notes (see table 3.6).

Finally, the agreement included the reopening of a debt/ equity swap program, which to avoid the disadvantages of the previous experience is limited in the amount of debt

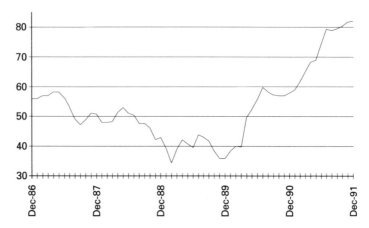

Figure 3.4
Secondary market price of the Mexican debt (cents on the dollar)
Source: Office of the Treasurer for Foreign Exchange Operations, Banco
de México.
1) Before March 1990 refers to the price of the UMS. After that date is the
price of the "new money" bonds.

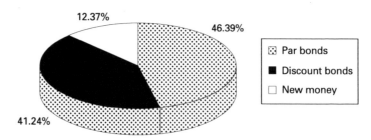

Figure 3.5
Structure of the response of commercial banks to the menu put forward
by Mexico and the Bank Advisory Committee
Source: SAFI, Ministry of Finance.

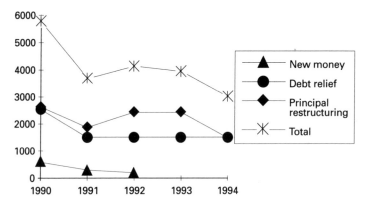

Figure 3.6
Reduction in service flows resulting from the agreement with commercial banks (million US$)
Source: SAFI, Ministry of Finance.

subject to auction, the use of the proceeds from a swap operation, and the time during which these swaps may take place. Specifically, the program allowed the cancellation of $3,500 million of "original" debt, and would be used exclusively for infrastructure projects approved by the federal government and/or for the purchase of public enterprises subject to privatization.

In conclusion, the process of adjustment and debt renegotiation that began in 1982 and ended with the signing of the agreement with commercial banks on 4 February 1990 has not only reopened access to voluntary external financing for public and private entities, but it has also cleared the way to think about other necessary measures such as deregulation, privatization, and social policies. During this time span, the "deleveraging" of the economy has been remarkable: total public sector debt has fallen from 80.5 percent of GDP in 1987 to about 46 percent in 1991. While

Table 3.6
Selected Mexican issues in the financial markets[1]

Issuer	Date	Type	Amount (millions)
BNCE	06/15/89	Notes	$100
TELMEX	07/06/90	Notes	$150
NAFIN	08/02/90	Notes	$100
PEMEX	10/25/90	Notes	$150
PEMEX	10/07/90	Notes	$100
PEMEX	04/24/90	Notes	DM100
Cemex	06/14/90	Convertible	$100
Cemex	10/17/89	Guaranteed notes	$150
PEMEX	07/20/90	Notes	Austrian sch. 500
Dyneworld	01/05/91	Notes	$100
PEMEX	03/04/91	Notes	$100
UMS	02/06/91	Notes	DM300
TELMEX	05/10/91	Notes	$570
Cemex	05/12/91	Guaranteed notes	$425
PEMEX	08/20/91	Notes	ECU100
UMS	08/25/91	Notes	Ptas 10bn.
Cemex	10/10/91	Medium-term notes	$100
BNCE	04/18/91	Medium-term notes	$100
NAFIN	06/09/91	Medium-term notes	$200
Soc. Fomento. Indust.	08/06/91	Euro comm. paper	$100
Cemex	08/30/91	Euro comm. paper	$100

Source: Nacional Financiera.
1. Includes only those above $100 million or the first issues in a nondollar currency.

gross internal debt has dropped from 23.1 percent in 1987 to 18.1 percent in 1991, net external debt has shown the most impressive decrease, finally from 57.4 percent of GDP in 1987 to just 27.7 percent in 1991. Concurrently, the servicing costs of the total external debt have declined considerably, with interest payments in the first half of 1991 representing only 18.5 percent as a proportion of exports of goods and services, down from 43.6 percent in 1982 (see figure 3.7).

1.4 Ten Thoughts on the Renegotiation of the External Debt

As I have done in previous sections, I would like to close with some reflections on what we have learned from the years of debt overhang and renegotiation.

1. *External debt management cannot substitute for sound economic policy.* Structural disequilibria can only be corrected through comprehensive structural adjustments; external debt management cannot be a substitute. Actually, a comprehensive structural adjustment is a prerequisite to attaining a successful external debt negotiation, which in turn consolidates the benefits of such sound policies. The Mexican experience over ten years of debt management has proved that the larger and deeper the structural reform efforts, the better the terms and conditions obtained in the negotiations.

2. *International consensus is crucial to solving the debt problem.* Given an adequate international political, economic, and financial environment, intensive work is still required to convince international financial institutions, creditors, and their governments, as well as public opinion makers such as academics and journalists, that the debtor country has

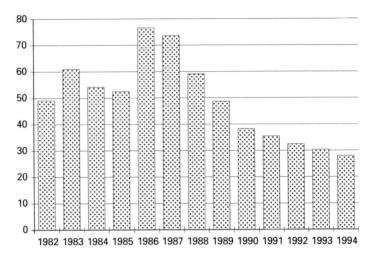

Figure 3.7
Total economic external debt as percentage of GDP
Source: SAFI, Ministry of Finance.

exhausted all available efforts and therefore needs international support.

3. Sovereign debt negotiation is not a debtor-creditor issue. Negotiation should be considered as a global issue that involves the entire international financial community and governments. This has an inherent political dimension, and a solution can only be achieved through the participation of all concerned parties.

4. Confrontation only obstructs a satisfactory, long-lasting solution to debt problems. Although defense of national interest is a sovereign right that justifies unilateral decisions, debt repudiation as a negotiating strategy can only bring ephemeral relief. Furthermore, it leads to financial isolation and increased uncertainty, and in the end works against the debtor's national interest.

5. Debtor clubs can offer only minimal common-denominator solutions. Given that different countries face different problems under different circumstances, block negotiations benefits are limited by the worst-performance country.

6. Negotiation packages must be as ample and flexible as possible. Given the diversity of creditor countries' legal, fiscal, and administrative frameworks, creditor banks must be offered a wide spectrum of viable options from which to choose. These options, however, should be financially equivalent in present value.

7. A timely satisfactory agreement is better than an optimal but extemporaneous one. Time is of the essence in the debt negotiation process. A timely solution is better than further improvements in the terms and conditions, which at the margin are time-consuming and do not offset the cost of the increased uncertainty generated by the delay of the settlement.

8. A far-reaching solution must be attained. As important as the agreement itself are the expectations that it generates. However, the desired expectations can only be derived from a comprehensive negotiation package that involves an amount of debt perceived by economic agents as being enough to bring a permanent and irreversible solution. This leads to a series of important indirect benefits such as a reduction in domestic interest rates, capital repatriation, foreign investment attraction, and voluntary access to international capital markets, which multiply the gains of the agreement.

9. There is no unique parameter with which to evaluate negotiations results. As each country has its own needs, it has to determine what is a good agreement. What is sufficient for one country may not be so for another.

10. There is life after debt. A sound economic policy is necessary to attain a successful negotiation, which leads to the creation of a virtuous circle. Such negotiation acts as a catalyst to structural reforms and leads to increased confidence, higher investments, lower inflation, and higher growth.

2 The Trade Liberalization Program

2.1 Background

Protectionist measures, mostly in the form of import tariffs, have a long history in Mexico. Until World War II, however, they focused on specific products. Only after the war, when competition from abroad regained its former strength, did a more comprehensive system of protection come into being, mainly to give the newly emerging manufacturing industry a chance to grow and prosper.

During the 1950s the principal aim of Mexican foreign trade policies was to substitute imports of final consumption goods. After a reasonably successful initial period, the possibilities for a continued substitution of those goods were virtually exhausted, and during the 1960s attention gradually turned to the substitution of intermediate manufactures. It was hoped that the process would lead to further vertical integration of the domestic industrial sector. Parallel to this development, there had been an important effort to prevent the export of unprocessed raw materials. In imposing moderate taxes on the export of unprocessed agricultural and mineral products, the intention was to stimulate processing within Mexico.

By 1970, these policies had led to a situation characterized by a slightly negative protection of primary activities, a moderate protection of intermediate manufactures, and a considerably strong protection of consumer durables.[21] During the 1970s, foreign trade policies became increasingly dictated by balance of payments considerations, and although the basic protectionist structure did not change, import policies were tightened under the administration of President Echeverría in an attempt to control the growing external deficits that ultimately led to the 1976 devaluation.

With inflation gradually increasing from 16 percent a year in 1978 to almost 30 percent in 1980, Mexican price controls and subsidies were directed toward keeping the prices of foodstuffs and other popular nondurables at a low level. This meant that for a number of basic subsistence crops— wheat, beans, and rice, among others—import prices were well above controlled domestic prices. To guarantee sufficient domestic supply at controlled prices, huge quantities were imported by the state-owned company CONASUPO, and the gap between import and domestic retail prices grew wider.

Official pricing policies also predominated in the energy sector. One of the ways the Mexican authorities attempted to make oil resources benefit national economic development was to make energy available at prices far below those governing international markets. Clearly, such pricing policies had to be complemented by trade policies, such as export regulations to prevent cheap fuels from being exported directly and import subsidies in case of insufficient domestic supply for most basic petrochemicals.

By the beginning of the 1980s, these measures had led to a very distorted price structure. Although the average nominal protection was around zero,[22] in fact there was a strongly negative protection for petroleum-derived products, a negative protection for most goods subject to some form of price control, and a somewhat positive protection for the majority of the uncontrolled goods. These distortions were exacerbated by the conspicuous use of nontariff barriers such as quotas encompassing practically all foreign trade, and the use of official prices for customs appraisals.

During 1981, as a result of the worsening of the terms of trade, the authorities responded with an elevation of the nominal rates of protection, bringing the average to around 10 percent before the devaluations of 1982. Although this was followed by variations in the average level of protection, which stayed in line with the fluctuations of the real exchange rate, the basic structure of protection remained essentially unchanged.

By the end of 1985, the Mexican authorities began a profound process of deregulation and trade opening, which continues today. The measures have included a drastic reduction in the levels and dispersion of tariffs, the nearly total elimination of quantitative trade restrictions, and intensive bilateral negotiations conducive to signing free trade agreements with Mexico's major trading partners.

Before going into detail on how this drastic change in policy direction is taking place in practice, I would like to use the next section to reflect, with the help of a very simple growth model, on the effects of micropolicies on macroaggregates, by referring to the specific case of the opening of the Mexican economy in 1985.

2.2 On the Economic Effects of Trade Liberalization and Economic Deregulation

One of the most important obstacles to the process of microeconomic reform is that its effects are mostly qualitative, spreading over markets through time, whereas monetary and fiscal measures usually have immediate effects on specific variables such as interest rates or the rate of inflation. Consequently, in many instances it is difficult to justify—beyond purely theoretical and even ideological grounds—an extensive program of opening up of the economy, which would affect special interest groups. Nevertheless, in the case of Mexico, the depth and persistence of the crisis suggested that the impact on resource allocation of revamping the prevailing regulation could be significant.

Although it is very complicated to talk about aggregate numbers when dealing with microeconomic issues, one can always try to work with simple models to get a preliminary sense of the orders of magnitude. The simplest exercise, described in the appendix to this chapter, would be to try to gauge where the economy is—given the technology and available resources—compared to a notional optimum in a closed and in an open economy. Thinking in very simple terms, the idea is to compare three points on a graph: the actual production level of the economy, the point on the transformation curve that maximizes net output at domestic prices, and the solution that maximizes net production at international prices. The constraints of the model would be given by the availability of foreign exchange, the stock of capital, and the preferences of consumers, which are assumed to be given by a Cobb-Douglas utility function. Finally, to capture some of the dynamics of structural change, it is presented as a six-period, twelve-sector model. Calculated with information on the structure of the economy in 1985,[23] it was found that the observed "vector" of production and consumption is significantly far from the "optimal vector" calculated by the model. In fact, the model predicts that during a six-year interval, derived only from an improved allocation of investment, there would be a catching-up process that would make it possible to grow at an average annual rate of 6.6 percent during the planning horizon, even with a foreign exchange constraint equivalent to average negative net transfers of 6 percent of GDP. This rate of growth, compared with the average rate of growth registered between 1984 and 1990[24] of around 2.5 percent, would mean that with the same initial conditions regarding available capital and foreign exchange resources, it would be possible to find an allocation capable of generating 25 percent more output after six years, provided that full employment of labor or land were not reached before then.

When comparing the optimal closed economy solution with the optimal open economy solution (that is, when comparing the vector obtained when maximizing net production at the current relative price structure to that obtained using international prices), the difference between aggregate solutions is much smaller. The present value of net production and consumption flows in both cases does not differ by more than half of a percentage point (see table 3.7).

In spite of the fact that aggregate production and consumption in the open and closed economy models differ very little, the composition of output by the end of the planning horizon already shows important changes. As illustrated in table 3.7, the optimal open economy model shows essentially less production of oil and more production of automobiles than in the closed economy. These changes could translate into higher long-term exports and higher growth; according to the model, however, these effects would not be significantly reflected in the aggregated figures until some time beyond the end of the optimization period.

These three results can lead to the interesting conclusion that, as has been seen in other exercises of trade liberali-

Table 3.7
Comparison of optimal production in a closed and in an open economy

Sector	Value of gross output in open economy/closed economy (%)[1]
Agriculture, livestock, and fishing	0.88
Mining	8.86
Oil and natural gas	−14.2
Processed foodstuffs	−0.28
Textiles and clothing	−0.50
Chemical products	13.7
Wood and cement	4.17
Appliances, machinery, and equipment	14.6
Automobiles and other transport equipment	27.4
Building industry	17.6
Electricity	3.33
Commerce and services	3.00

1. On the terminal period.

zation,[25] the relative price correction coming from the harmonization and reduction of tariff levels does not necessarily translate into dramatic improvements in production and economic welfare, even in the medium term. Rather, when trade liberalization opens the way to other forms of economic deregulation that foster internal as well as international competition, the economic impact can be considerable.

The intuition behind this kind of outcome has been supported by the international evidence on competitive advantage,[26] which shows a stronger performance of those developing countries that are more outward-oriented in their trade strategies. Parallel is the view that import-substitution strategies have not worked as well as expected in the 1950s and 1960s.[27] Therefore, although trade liberalization can be one of the most eye-catching areas of reform, it will fail to enhance the economic potential of the economy if it is not accompanied by a much more comprehensive set of microeconomic and macroeconomic deregulation reforms in the industrial, commercial, and primary sectors.[28]

2.3 The Trade Liberalization Program

The elimination of nontariff barriers and reduction of tariffs has taken place in three stages. The first involved two important policies adopted in 1985. It was decided that Mexico would unilaterally eliminate import permits on almost 80 percent of the tariff items subject to quantitative restrictions, and then begin a gradual process of phasing out the remaining quotas. In November the country started negotiating for admission to the General Agreement on Tariffs and Trade (GATT), and became a full member in July 1986. As a result of this first move toward trade liberalization, by the end of the year less than 28 percent of the value of imports was subject to quotas, compared with 83 percent at the beginning of 1985. The weighted tariff level was brought down from 16.4 percent to 13.1 percent, and dispersion was reduced from 16 to 11 tariffs.

The second stage is directly connected with the implementation of the Economic Pact for Economic Stability, as described in chapter 1. At the time, on top of the favorable structural effects of a more rational protection strategy, it was envisaged that external competition would also contribute to the effort to stabilize inflation. It was therefore decided that the policy of liberalization already in process should be significantly speeded up as an integral part of the stabilization program. Between December 1987 and December 1988, the maximum tariff was brought down from 100 percent to 20 percent, and the number of items subject to quantitative restrictions from 1,200 to 325, representing 21.2 percent of total imports. During 1989, 13 more items were excluded from the schedule of quota restrictions, and 106 more were excluded during 1990.

By year-end 1991, less than 10 percent of the total value of imports is subject to import licensing—the lowest level in thirty-six years. Regarding composition, 54 percent of imports subject to licenses correspond to agricultural products, 11 percent to petroleum products, 23 percent to inputs in the capital good industry, 7 percent to the automobile industry, and the remaining 5 percent to items from the electronic, chemical, and pharmaceutical industries (see table 3.8).

As part of the liberalization scheme, all "official prices" used for customs appraisals, which applied to 41 tariff categories, were eliminated during the first months of 1988

Table 3.8
Value of imports subject to permits

	Percentage
1983	100.0
1984	83.0
1985	35.1
1986	27.8
1987	26.8
1988	21.2
1989	18.4
1990	13.7
1991	9.1

Source: SECOFI

and replaced by the adoption of antidumping legislation in accordance with GATT rules and a system of countervailing duties (see table 3.9). With respect to tariff levels, the number of applicable duty categories was trimmed to five by the end of 1987, taking the maximum tariff to 20 percent, with a further reduction in dispersion in 1989, when the minimum tariff for a significant number of products was raised to 10 percent. Thus during last year more than 20 percent of the total value of imports entered the country duty free, with the remaining portion subject to rates between 5 and 20 percent.

The third stage in the process of trade reform has been marked by strengthened bilateral relations with our major trading partners. In 1985, Mexico and the United States signed a bilateral agreement on subsidies and countervailing duties, by virtue of which American firms had to prove that injury had been caused *before* applying the duty. In 1987, both countries signed a framework agreement to set up principles and procedures for resolving controversies on trade and investment. In October 1989, a new framework agreement was signed to start global conversations to facilitate trade and investment. By March 1990, trade and

Table 3.9
Tariff structure

	1982	1986	1989	1990	1991
Number of items	8,008	8,206	11,838	11,817	11,812
Average tariff (%)	27.0	22.6	13.1	13.1	13.1
Weighted average tariff (%)	16.4	13.1	9.7	10.5	11.1
Number of rates	16	11	5	5	5
Maximum tariff (%)	100	100	20	20	20

Source: SECOFI.

investment relations with Canada were ruled by the Trade Agreement of 1946, the Agreement on Industry and Energy Cooperation, and the Memorandum of Understanding on Trade-Related Issues of 1984.

On 11 June 1990, Presidents Salinas and Bush decided to instruct their respective ministries of trade to start working on a free trade agreement, and in the following months Canada joined the process. To date the negotiation has focused on six areas of dicussion. The first deals with aspects of *market access*, including tariffs and nontariff barriers, rules of origin, government purchases, agriculture, the automobile industry, and other industries. The second deals with *trade regulations* such as standards, subsidies, and antidumping measures. The third is concerned with *services* in the financial and insurance sectors, ground transportation, telecommunications, and others. The fourth focuses on *investment,* the fifth on *patents and intellectual property,* and the sixth area involves the solution of *controversies.* When completed, the treaty will promote the creation of a free trade area with a combined output of $6 trillion and a market of more than 360 million people.

At the same time, Mexico has also been negotiating free trade agreements with other major trading partners. For instance, last September the first free trade treaty was signed with the government of Chile, and similar agreements are now being negotiated with Venezuela, Colombia, and the Central American countries (see table 3.10).

2.4 Ten Practical Considerations on Trade Liberalization

The opening up of the economy can be a very effective way of inducing economic efficiency, to the extent that the sequencing and the macroeconomic context in which it

Table 3.10
Mexico's major trading partners (1990)

	% Exports	% Imports
United States	69.7	64.6
Canada	0.9	1.5
ALADI	3.2	4.1
Central American Common Market	1.6	0.3
EEC	12.7	15.6
EFTA	0.9	2.6
Japan	5.6	4.7
Other Asian countries	2.3	3.9
Rest of the world	3.1	2.7

Source: Banco de México, *The Mexican Economy in 1991.*

happens creates the right environment for firms to adapt promptly to the new competitive conditions. The experience arising out of the implementation of trade liberalization policies in Mexico can be summarized by mentioning some of the lessons learned.

1. *Trade liberalization plays a central role in the stabilization strategy.* While aggregate demand management discipline and consensus-gathering negotiations are at the center of inflation reduction in the nontradable goods sector, the dynamics of tradable goods prices are essentially determined by the exchange rate and trade policies. Having an open economy enhances the impact of monetary restraint and therefore becomes an indispensable element of the overall stabilization strategy.

2. *The opening up of the economy has to be supported also by strong macroeconomic fundamentals.* Conversely, liberalization is also supported by other macroeconomic policies. In

fact, pursuing liberalization in an overheated economy can only lead to further balance of payments problems. To allow the change in relative prices implied by the elimination and/ or reduction of tariffs and nontariff barriers to play its allocational purpose, it is necessary to have a stable economy where markets can carry price signals adequately.

3. In addition to a strict fiscal discipline, it is best to start the trade liberalization process with a depreciated real exchange rate. It can be useful to open up the economy and simultaneously back the measure with a change in the real exchange rate. Firms will then have the room and the time to adapt to the new rules of the game. If, on the contrary, protection is eliminated with an appreciated exchange rate, it is likely that this measure will make the balance of payments problems even worse. Many companies may be forced out of business before they have the chance to become more efficient and competitive.

4. The first phase of trade liberalization has to be comprehensive and put in place rapidly. The first stage in the liberalization process has to include all sectors of the economy. It also must be implemented as quickly as possible to remain ahead of the resistance offered by groups of inefficient producers in previously overprotected sectors whose interests are going to be affected by the measures.

5. The liberalization process has to start with the elimination of nontariff barriers. Then it can go for a reduction in the level and dispersion of tariffs. In practice, it is the bulk of nontariff barriers that makes the protection system extremely complicated, obscure, and discretionary. Also, most of the resistance from interest groups will center on import quotas and other ad hoc regulations. Once they have been removed, it will be easier to reduce their dispersion and level. In this way the effect of changes in tariff policy will also be easier to evaluate in the context of the rest of the fiscal and exchange rate policies.

6. Tariffs should not be viewed solely as sources of fiscal revenues. Even though tariffs can represent an important source of revenues, trade liberalization policy should not be dominated by its fiscal impact. More efficient means of taxation can be used to compensate for the eventual revenue losses. In contrast, tariffs have to be evaluated in terms of the effects that they have on overall economic efficiency.

7. Usually the first stage of tariff reduction has to be unilateral. The first part of the process of liberalization, which includes the elimination of nontariff barriers and the reduction in the level and dispersion of tariffs, usually has to be unilateral. The use of multilateral means, such as the GATT or the negotiation of free trade agreements, is not intended for exchanging big concessions, but mainly for looking at the "fine tuning" of commercial regulations. In consequence, having an already leaner protection system is in practice a precondition for further progress in terms of participation in the global economy.

8. If the neighboring country has a strong economy, nontariff protection is not only distortionary, but it can foster corruption and smuggling. When, as in the case of Mexico, a country shares a long border with a large industrial country, nontariff barriers will commonly fail to protect the industries they are supposed to promote because smuggling is easy. In contrast, if permits are substituted for tariffs, it is probable that formerly illegal imports will begin to yield taxes as they enter the country legally.

9. Trade liberalization has to be fair. The liberalization process has to be fair. Fairness in this context means three things: first, if private enterprises are going to be exposed to international competition, the same must apply to public enterprises. Having a double standard in this area will not only translate into the survival of costly, inefficient parastatal firms, it will also create distortions, implying that resources will be deviated from alternative uses by more efficient firms. Second, trade liberalization cannot be a unilateral process permanently. To reach the goals of increasing competitiveness and reap the benefits of specialization, trade liberalization has to occur on a bilateral and multilateral basis as in the case of a free trade agreement. Finally, trade relations have to take place on an equal footing for competitors on both sides of the border. Dumping and other unfair trade practices end up neutralizing the intended benefits from the elimination of tariff and nontariff barriers.

10. Trade liberalization should be seen as part of an even wider program of structural reform. Trade liberalization alone is not a powerful enough tool to induce higher growth and better resource allocation. In fact, it should also be a part of a more comprehensive set of measures aimed at improving the general business environment, such as privatization, new rules for foreign investment, deregulation of overregulated sectors, and antitrust policy, among others.

3 Direct Foreign Investment

3.1 Background

The roles of foreign investment and multinational corporations have long been a matter of debate regarding Mexico's industrial policy. In practice, the measures adopted to promote industrialization for most of this century have been characterized by a reticent approach toward foreign ownership, based on a fear of the possible loss of sovereignty.

Although the size and fragmentation of Mexican markets give reason to fear the formation of monopolies, time has suggested that the overprotective foreign investment regulations were essentially addressing the right question with the wrong instrument. In fact, it could be said that the lack of a more comprehensive approach to the issue of market competition precluded greater participation of foreign capital in Mexico's development program.

The two most notable instances of foreign investment legislation in Mexico have been the presidential decree issued in 1944, which gave the government discretionary authority to require 51 percent Mexican ownership in all Mexican companies, and the 1972 Law to Promote Mexican Investment and Regulate Foreign Investment, which confirmed the principles outlined in the previous decree but had very ambiguous definitions regarding which sectors would actually be subject to such limits, leaving the way open for discretionary application of the rules.

Looking at foreign investment in Mexico during the last twenty years, one can find ample evidence of its great potential in a *complementary* role, both in terms of macroeconomic balances and allocational efficiency (see table 3.11 and figure 3.8). For example, detailed studies of the industrial sector aimed at testing Gerschenkron's theory of convergence led to four interesting observations. First, productivity levels of locally owned firms have converged with those of foreign-owned firms. Second, the rate of productivity growth of local firms and how rapidly they catch up with multinationals are positively related to the degree of foreign ownership of an industry. Third, the productivity gap between Mexican and U.S. manufacturing sectors between the mid-1960s and mid-1980s has diminished.

Table 3.11
Total foreign investment ($U.S. millions)[1]

Year	New investment	Cumulative
1973	287.3	4,359.5
1974	362.2	4,721.7
1975	295.0	5,016.7
1976	299.1	5,315.8
1977	327.1	5,642.9
1978	383.3	6,026.2
1979	810.0	6,836.2
1980	1,622.6	8,458.8
1981	1,701.1	10,159.9
1982	626.5	10,786.4
1983	683.7	11,470.1
1984	1,442.2	12,899.9
1985	1,871.0	14,628.9
1986	2,424.2	17,053.1
1987	3,877.2	20,930.3
1988	2,157.1	24,087.4
1989	2,913.7	27,001.1
1990	4,978.4	35,473.5
1991	9,414.6	44,888.2

Source: SECOFI, and the Securities and Exchange Commission.
1. Includes portfolio investment.

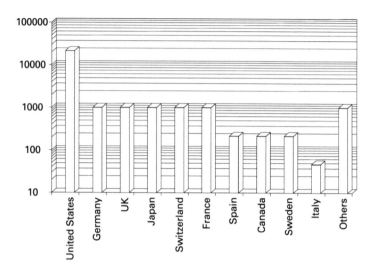

Figure 3.8
Cumulative foreign investment by country (million dollars)
Source: DGIE, Secofi.
1) Semi-log scale.

Fourth, the rate of productivity growth of Mexican industries and its rate of convergence with the United States are higher in industries with a greater presence of foreign investment.

Since the supporting regulation to the 1972 Law was issued (16 May 1989), and following the successful culmination of the debt renegotiation, there has been a very favorable evolution of foreign investment flows. These flows have also accelerated as a result of the business opportunities foreseen in the formation of a North American free trade area. For example, in 1991 the flows of foreign investment are expected to have reached nearly $10 billion, which is the largest amount ever recorded.

3.2 Outline of the Reform

The supplemental regulation to the 1972 Law provides a clear and nondiscretionary framework that favors the development of projects involving the transfer of technology, the generation of net foreign exchange earnings, and the creation of employment. Favorable consideration is also given to investments that contribute to the decentralization of economic activity and high rates of capital formation.

Foreign investors are authorized to establish new businesses in Mexico and may hold up to a 100 percent stake in "unrestricted" economic activities. Taken together, these activities represent approximately 66 percent of GDP, including food, beverages and tobacco, textiles, clothing, leather, wood and paper products, restaurants, hotels, and commerce. Most of these "unrestricted" sectors are no longer required to submit their projects for formal review and approval by the National Commission of Foreign Investment (CNIE). Approval can also become automatic upon registration with the National Registry of Foreign Investment, provided the project meets the following criteria:

a. Investment in fixed assets at the beginning of operations does not exceed the peso equivalent of U.S.$100 million.

b. Industrial projects are located outside of Mexico's three largest metropolitan areas: Mexico City, Guadalajara, and Monterrey.

c. The company maintains an overall positive balance in foreign exchange during its first three years of operation.

d. The investment has the potential to create permanent jobs and to establish worker training and development programs.

e. The project uses clean technology, which complies with environmental requirements.

Projects that do not meet these criteria are required to obtain prior authorization from the CNIE, but approval is automatic if a formal response is not received from the commission within forty-five working days of the date of application.

To avoid the discretionary application of these criteria, the 1989 regulations now clearly establish certain limitations to foreign investment by defining the following six regimes:

a. Activities exclusively reserved for the state (twelve activities), including the extraction of petroleum and natural gas, petroleum refining, the sale of electricity, telegraph services, railways, and the minting of coins.

b. Activities reserved for Mexicans (thirty-four activities), including the private broadcasting of radio programs, broadcasting and repetition of television programs, ground freight transportation, and ground passenger transportation services.

c. Activities in which foreign investment of up to 34 percent of the capital stock is permitted (four activities): including carbon mining and extraction and/or refining of sulfur, phosphoric rock, and ferrous minerals.

d. Activities in which foreign investment of up to 40 percent of capital stock is permitted (eight activities), including mainly secondary petrochemicals.

e. Activities in which foreign investment of up to 49 percent of the capital stock is permitted (twenty-five activities), including fishing, mining (excluding those activities listed in groups a and c), telephone services, insurance, and finance leasing companies.

f. Activities in which the Mexican foreign investment commission's prior approval is required for foreign investors to hold a majority interest (fifty-eight activities), such as agriculture, livestock and cattle raising, printing, editing and associated industries, construction, and educational services.

The 1989 reforms also allow foreigners to undertake portfolio investments in Mexican equities through special thirty-year trust funds. These trust funds are empowered to acquire and hold specially designated "N," or neutral, shares of Mexican corporations. These shares give foreign investors the same patrimonial rights as local investors, but not the same voting rights. This scheme has given Mexican companies the opportunity to raise further capital resources.

3.3. Other Areas of Economic Deregulation

The two most important areas of economic deregulation are related to trade and foreign investment. Nevertheless, the process of microeconomic reform involves a long, detailed series of studies and decisions made sector by sector, and in many ways one is as important as the other. This is why it may be interesting to list some other areas in which the elimination of excessive regulations and restrictions are intended to improve the competitive environment of the economy, and thus exploit more fully the *competitive advantages* of Mexico. In fact, what has been achieved through the various microeconomic reforms constitutes an important basis for future improvement in resource allocation and factor productivity, making it possible in the end to improve the standards of living of the population.

Technology, Patents, and Trademarks
The elimination of barriers to technology and the promotion of technological modernization has been pursued through new regulation, to replace a framework that greatly restricted the contractual freedom of Mexican companies in the purchase of technology. Last June, Congress passed a new, "state of the art" Law for the Protection and Promotion of Industrial Property. The most important changes were the allocation of patents to new technologies not previously taken into account, such as biotechnology. The life of the patents would extend twenty years from the date of presentation of the application. The authorization for the use of an already accredited license would be restricted to cases of grave shortage. A ten-year, renewable protection for trademarks simplified rules for the setting up of franchise agreements, and a national Institute of Industrial Property for supervision and registry was also created.

Communications and Transportation
The new resolutions grant freedom for the transportation of any kind of cargo (except for explosive and toxic substances) on federal roads, as well as for loading and unloading at any site. In addition, a surcharge on the transportation of imported goods has been eliminated. The authorities have implemented a program of concessions for the private construction and operation of toll roads and bridges. Furthemore, regional air transportation is being totally deregulated to open the way for small carriers.

Automobile Industry
Regulations imposing patterns of production, national content requirements, import substitution, selection of suppliers, models, and lines, foreign participation, and bans on certain imports have been eliminated. The new policy

replaces the above restrictions with two conditions: a trade balance in equilibrium and limitations on the vertical integration in the production of finished vehicles. In the case of the auto parts industry, restrictions concerning the origin of capital have also been eliminated.

Telecommunications
Operation is permitted without the need for prior authorization on advanced telecommunication equipment such as fax, telex, telephone exchanges, and multiline equipment. The consumer is free to buy from any supplier equipment previously sold only by Teléfonos de México. The licensing agreement of TELMEX mentioned in the previous chapter is also a central element of the new regulatory environment for telecommunications.

Aquaculture and Fisheries
Recent reforms provide that aquaculture on private premises does not require a license from the government. Instead, the only requirements are a notification of the start of operations and fulfillment of sanitary regulations.

Textiles
All decrees establishing the need for authorization to open and/or to enlarge a textile factory were abrogated.

Petrochemicals
Formerly, permits for the production of certain petrochemicals were granted on a discretionary basis and without clear rules, thereby discouraging investment. Now the list of primary and secondary petrochemicals is explicit. On the basis of technical criteria, twenty products are classified as primary petrochemicals instead of the thirty-four previously considered. Similarly, the list of secondary petro-

chemicals was reduced from eight hundred to sixty-six. Petrochemical permits are to be granted within forty-five days. Also, operating conditions for refining by-products were modified, eliminating the previous permit and establishing only the obligation to provide commercial information.

Electricity
Some types of high-tension electricity for industrial use can now be privately generated, as long as surplus production is sold to the grid.

4 Concluding Remarks

Internal adjustment and the breaking of the foreign exchange constraint are preconditions for further reform. It is not possible to start talking about privatization or social programs if there is no certainty about deficits and inflation. Furthermore, a developing country cannot maintain negative net transfers abroad for very long. As Angel Gurría, Deputy Minister of Finance for International Affairs, once said, the important thing is to resolve the debt problem as soon as possible and start concentrating on the fundamental issues of economic policy behind a sustainable process of development; after all, there has to be "life after debt."

Appendix A: A Simple Multi-Sector Dynamic Programming Model of the Mexican Economy

1. Sectors

(1) Agriculture, livestock, fishing.
(2) Mining.

(3)   Oil and natural gas.

(4)   Food.

(5)   Textiles and clothing.

(6)   Chemical products.

(7)   Wood and cement.

(8)   Appliances, machinery, and equipment.

(9)   Automobiles and other transport equipment.

(10) Building industry.

(11) Electricity.

(12) Commerce and services.

2. Definitions

Dimension

I   Sector of origin: 1, . . . , 12.

J   Sector of destination: 1, . . . , 12.

T   Time: 1, . . . , 6.

Scalars

IC   Technical coefficient for imports of consumption goods.

C0   Consumption-output ratio in 1985. Calculated from the national accounts.

FDI Net external savings to GDP. For this model the definition corresponds to the average current account deficit for the period 1982–1988, excluding 1986.

Vectors

CAP(I)   Output-capital ratio. From the capital flows and stock survey (values for 1985).

IM(I)   Technical coefficients for imports of
           intermediates.

IK(I)   Technical coefficients for imports of capital
           goods.

E(I)   Export-output ratio.

BETA(T)   Discount vector. Using a social rate of discount
           of 5.5 percent.

PROT(T)   Vector to transform domestic prices into
           international prices (prot*domestic =
           international). Prepared with information
           provided by SECOFI.

DEPR(I)   Rate of depreciation of capital stock in sector I,
           computed using information from the capital
           flows and stocks survey by Banco de México
           (values for 1985).

CON(I)   Proportions of total consumer budget spent on
           each good (Cobb-Douglas assumption).

Matrices

A(I,J)   Input-output matrix prepared with the 1985
           matrix provided by INEGI.

B(I,J)   Matrix of capital coefficients prepared with data
           from the survey on stock and flows of capital by
           Banco de México (values for 1985).

M(T,T)   Triangular matrix with ones in the upper
           triangle, and zeros elsewhere.

K(I,T)   Initial capital stock (in millions of pesos of 1985).

Variables

X(I,T)	Production of sector I in period T.
CONS(I,T)	Total consumption (public and private) of good I in period T.
V(I,T)	Increase of capacity in sector I in period T.
EXPO(I,T)	Exports from sector I in period T.
IMC(I,T)	Imports of consumption goods of type I in period T.
IMM(I,T)	Imports of intermediate goods by sector I in period T.
IMK(I,T)	Imports of capital goods by sector I in period T.
KA(I,T)	Capacity in sector I in period T.
MIPP(I,T)	Use of intermediates in production.
MCC(I,T)	Use of domestic production in investment.
IMPOR(I,T)	Total imports.
INTL(T)	Gross national product valued at international prices.
C(T)	Total consumption spending (public and private, both in domestic and imported goods and services).
W	Objective function.
NO-NEGATIVITY CONDITIONS	All variables are positive.

3. Equations[29]

(1) $X(I,T) \leq CAP(I)^*KA(I,T);$

(2) $CONS(I,T) + EXPO(I,T) + MIPP(I,T) + MCC(I,T) - X(I,T) \leq 0;$

(3) $IMPOR(I,T) = IMM(I,T) + IMK(I,T);$

(4) $IMM(I,T) = IM(I)^*X(I,T);$

(5) $IMK(I,T) = IK(I)^*V(I,T);$

(6) $IMC(T) = IC^*C(T);$

(7) $MIPP(I,T) = A(I,J)^*X(I,T);$

(8) $MCC(I,T) = B(I,J)^*V(I,T);$

(9) $PROT(I)^*CONS(I,T) = CON(I)^*C(T);$

(10) $KA(I,T) = SUM(t \leq T, V(I,T)^*M(T,T)) - DEPR(I)^*KA(I,T-1)$

(11) $SUM(I,EXPO(I,T)) - SUM(I,IMPOR(I,T)) - IMC(T) \geq -FDI^*INTL(T);$

(12) $C(T) \geq C0^*INTL(T);$

(13) $INTL(T) = SUM(I,PROT(I)^*X(I,T)) - SUM(I,PROT(I)^*MIPP(I,T));$

(14) $W = SUM(T,BETA(T)^*INTL(T)).$

4. Optimization Exercise

The exercise consists of maximizing equation (14) subject to conditions (1)–(13) and the non-negativity constraints. In the case of a closed economy PROT(I) is a unit vector, in the case of the open economy it is as described in the definitions.

4

Thoughts on the Mexican Privatization Experience

One of the most important elements in the strategy of adjustment and structural transformation of Mexico has been the divestiture of public sector enterprises. Seen as a necessary condition for a permanent correction of public sector finances and the development of an efficient productive base, the sale, liquidation, merger, or transfer of small public sector entities was begun by the authorities in 1983. This effort has continued with added intensity during the administration of President Salinas de Gortari, with the completion of larger and substantially more complex privatization operations.

During the last nine years, the government has divested itself from practically all areas of economic activity: from sugar mills to hotels, airlines, telecommunications, the banking sector, and the steel industry. Out of the 1,155 firms under state control in 1982, 905 enterprises, plus another 87 still under way, have been divested. This translates into cumulative sales of U.S. $14.5 billion (around 5 percent of GDP), and the transfer of a quarter of a million employees to the private sector by the end of 1991.

The purpose of this chapter is to describe this side of the Mexican experience by looking not only at the macroeconomic and allocative effects of privatization, but also at the institutional and financial constraints that have decisively influenced the characteristics of the scheme adopted in each particular case. To that effect, the chapter has been divided into three sections. The first provides background on the role of the state in the development process. Section 2 reviews the microeconomic and macroeconomic considerations that influenced each concrete strategy of privatization, and section 3 looks at how privatization has been carried out in practice.

1 Background: The Role of the State in the Mexican Economy

Throughout the development of postrevolutionary Mexico, the role of the state, as well as our understanding of what it should be, has changed substantially with the changing needs and external conditions of society. During the first years after the Revolution, Mexico was a very fragmented country, with an economy that had undergone serious material destruction and institutions that had to be rebuilt to support the model of the country envisioned by the new constitution.

Between 1920 and the years of the Great Depression, the institutional expansion of the public sector was essentially focused on the task of reconstruction, the creation of new infrastructure, and the provision of a framework that would allow private initiative to restart the process of investment and growth. To that effect the first parastatal entities were created to complement the administrative roles of the central government. They concentrated on specialized tasks, such as monetary control through the creation of the Banco de México, or the building of infrastructure by the National

Commission of Roads and Highways, and the National Commission of Irrigation.

As happened almost everywhere else, the worldwide economic crisis provided a strong argument for active state intervention in the economy. In 1934, President Cardenas presented to the nation the first six-year plan, which changed in a very profound way the idea of the responsibilities of the public sector. The plan guaranteed economic and social progress through a government policy based on three principles: direct control over national resources and strategic industries, the expansion of government spending, and the creation of new productive and social infrastructure. During this decade, the parastatal sector grew mainly in two areas: the organization of public enterprises to generate "basic" products, such as the National Commission of Electricity, and the creation of enterprises to administer already nationalized sectors such as Petróleos Mexicanos, and the National Railway Company. The state financial sector was filled out by the creation of a group of national development banks such as Nacional Financiera, several banks for agriculture financing, and the export-import bank.

During the war years and the following decade, the authorities continued to embrace the idea of a strong government directly involved in productive activities, but with a clearer sense of the limits of the state. Under the more global strategy of import-substitution industrialization, state enterprises would be in charge of providing a reliable flow of industrial raw materials to a nascent national private industry, which would be responsible for the production of final consumption goods. The state began to invest heavily in those activities that were very capital intensive and provided the basis of the productive chains. These included steel mills (Altos Hornos de México), fertilizers (Guanos y Fertilizantes), coal mines (Carbonífera de Pachuca), paper mills (Compañía Industrial de Atenquique y Ayutla), etc. Also in this period, new institutions such as the National Institute of Social Security (1943) and the National Institute for the Social Security of Government Employees (1949) were created to take over the social security system.

During the era of the *desarrollo estabilizador (1954–1970)*, the engine of the industrialization process gradually shifted from a rapid expansion of government investment to an increase in private (both domestic and foreign) investment. Private investment, however, was largely financed out of tax privileges and rents provided by an extensive arrangement of tariff and nontariff barriers, and by overregulation that prevented the free entry of producers into many markets. Then the government invested less, set up fewer new enterprises and kept a strong position on public finances to maintain low inflation. This arrangement worked very well until it became apparent that the import-substitution strategy could not sustain growth indefinitely. The rents of the protected internal market would be exhausted sooner or later, and the competitive structure implied by the strategy did not introduce the incentives to keep the economy moving forward through an increase in productivity.

Faced with the alternative of once again pushing up public investment or dismantling the constitutional obstacles to competition and private investment, Mexico entered the 1970s having opted for the former. Gradually, as private investment became less dynamic, the government took over the lead of the economy once again, spending more and obtaining most of the needed resources from external borrowing. During the first half of the decade, gigantic new companies were created or acquired, especially in the capital goods sector. These included SIDERMEX (steel), DINA (trucks and automobiles), CONCARRIL (trains), and PROPEMEX (fishing), to mention but a few (see table 4.1).

This explosive growth in the parastatal sector was further accelerated by the overall structural weakness of the economy in the last part of the 1970s. The large and rapid appreciation of the real exchange rate, the environment of high and unstable inflation, and distortions in the credit markets that resulted increasingly in credit rationing put many private firms on the brink of bankruptcy. In those years, the addition of new firms to the parastatal sector was not only the result of government industrial strategy, but also a massive rescue operation designed to save jobs. As a result, by the end of 1982 the parastatal sector comprising 1,155 firms—including all commercial banks—accounted for 18.5 percent of GDP[1] and employed nearly one million people, or 10 percent of total employment in the economy (see table 4.2).

Table 4.1
Evolution of the parastatal sector in Mexico (1920–1982)

	Net increase in the number of firms incorporated in the public sector	Cumulative number of parastatal firms at the end of the period
1920–1934	15	15
1935–1940	21	36
1941–1954	108	144
1955–1962	62	206
1963–1970	66	272
1971–1975	232	504
1976–1982	651	1,155

Source: Elaborated with information from SEMIP.

Table 4.2
Indicators of parastatal sector activities (% of GDP)

	Total public sector spending	Public investment[1]	Parastatal sector spending[2]	Parastatal sector revenues	Parastatal sector balance
1950	7.87	6.1			
1951	8.61	5.2			
1952	10.79	5.5			
1953	8.84	5.0			
1954	10.71	5.7			
1955	10.06	5.0			
1956	10.34	4.6			
1957	9.85	4.9			
1958	10.71	5.0			
1959	10.55	4.9			
1960	13.39	5.6			
1961	12.61	6.4			
1962	11.43	6.1			
1963	10.42	7.1			
1964	12.77	7.9			
1965	26.30	5.4	11.22	11.71	0.49
1966	24.39	5.7	12.39	12.32	−0.07
1967	26.36	7.0	12.81	12.92	0.11
1968	24.60	6.9	12.47	12.50	0.03
1969	26.14	7.0	12.85	12.98	0.12
1970	24.59	6.6	12.74	12.82	0.09
1971	24.77	4.6	13.38	13.40	0.03
1972	26.35	5.9	12.67	12.72	0.05
1973	29.54	7.2	14.73	14.87	0.14
1974	30.74	7.2	15.64	15.61	−0.02
1975	36.43	8.7	18.20	18.23	0.03
1976	37.94	7.9	17.88	17.63	−0.25
1977	29.96	7.6	12.25	12.02	−0.23
1978	31.22	8.7	13.41	12.77	−0.64
1979	32.67	9.8	13.65	13.47	−0.19

Table 4.2 (continued)

	Total public sector spending	Public investment[1]	Parastatal sector spending[2]	Parastatal sector revenues	Parastatal sector balance
1980	34.40	9.6	13.38	14.93	1.55
1981	40.93	12.9	15.98	14.81	−1.17
1982	47.24	10.2	14.24	18.01	3.77
1983	40.52	7.5	13.07	22.26	9.19
1984	38.81	6.7	13.59	22.33	8.73
1985	38.61	6.1	13.03	21.08	8.05
1986	43.97	6.0	13.73	19.42	5.69
1987	44.67	5.5	12.40	19.83	7.44
1988	40.03	4.4	11.73	18.04	6.31
1989	34.38	3.9	9.97	15.48	5.51
1990	28.51	5.0	10.50	15.50	5.00
1991	27.00	5.2	9.40	14.00	4.60

Source: Elaborated with information from Banco de México, Indicatores Económicos. La Economía Mexicana en Cifras, Nacional Financiera and Cuenta Pública, SPP, several issues.
1. Includes investment by noncontrolled parastatal entities.
2. The parastatal sector is incorporated in the budget of 1965.

2 The Economics of Privatization

2.1 Performance under Public and Private Ownership: A Review of the Theoretical Debate

Before talking specifically about privatization in Mexico, it might be useful to try to understand in which cases there is a rationale for public intervention and in which other circumstances there are not good reasons for keeping firms under state control. Starting from a purely theoretical standpoint—in a world with no indivisibilities or sunk costs, where it is costless and possible to write and enforce contracts as complicated as necessary, and where markets are complete and function reasonably well—there are no substantial grounds for claiming that the transfer from the public to the private sector (or vice versa) of entitlements to the control of the decisions and residual profits of an enterprise should have any significant effect on either economic efficiency or macroeconomic stability.

When a country begins its development process, it is possible to find strong reasons to have a widespread state presence in the economy. The lack of markets and infrastructure may present such insurmountable obstacles to private entrepreneurs that no one would be interested in producing certain types of goods—or if they were interested, there is no guarantee that they would do it efficiently. In fact, looking carefully at the literature and at the experience in other countries, one could come to the conclusion that there are basically three economic circumstances in which public ownership can be rationalized:

a. Missing markets and insufficient taxation. When a large proportion of transactions in a country are not carried out through well-organized markets, or taxes are difficult to collect, the profits of public firms can be an important source of noninflationary resources to finance infrastructure and social investment.

b. Prices vs. quantities in fragmented markets. It has been pointed out[2] that when one is to choose whether an economy has predominantly price signals or quantity signals, it is crucial to look at the dynamics and adjustment costs. In certain circumstances there is a trade-off between speed of response and efficiency. For instance, private firms using price signals could achieve a better allocation of resources in the end. In the case of certain external shocks, however, some time usually elapses between the moment at which the market transmits the new information to the agents and the moment at which they respond with changes in the quantities supplied. In some strategic industries, any episode of excess demand could be very disruptive to the rest of the economy. *Therefore, when adjustment costs are high, when there is a natural tendency to form monopolies, and when the industry plays a strategic role in the economy, public ownership may be the best alternative.* This is the case, for example, of the extraction of oil and the basic petrochemical industries.

c. Income distribution, natural monopolies, and market size. When the market size of the country is not large enough to support a strong competitive structure, and when the country lacks the legal framework, the institutions, and the experience to carry out an effective antitrust policy, it may be easier to use public enterprises instead of a complicated combination of taxation and regulatory measures to achieve economic efficiency and a fair distribution of income.[3]

The first and the third arguments for state ownership become less applicable as the construction of infrastructure links formerly separated markets, the advance in industrialization and foreign trade provides a more competitive environment, and the tax system matures.

The empirical literature of economic development, public choice theory, and industrial organization has highlighted some important shortcomings in the operation of parastatal companies, which can very seriously hurt the economy as a whole in terms of both efficiency and social justice.[4] Drawing from these studies, it could be said that in spite of the theoretical arguments in favor of widespread state intervention in less developed countries, in practice the circumstances under which state firms are created and managed make the benefits less obvious.

Efficiency
The process of formation of a parastatal sector is not always guided by some of the criteria mentioned above. In many instances, firms are incorporated at random to the public sector in an attempt to save jobs. The result is that the government ends up with cabarets, cinemas, airlines, and hotels, without any consistent strategy. Furthermore, many of the firms rescued by the governments are not efficient to begin with, which is why they were about to go bankrupt. In most cases the new government management does not improve the situation. Firms making losses usually keep on making losses, placing an additional burden on the taxpayers and worsening the overall macroeconomic picture.[5] In addition, the policy of rescuing inefficient firms introduces a negative incentive to private firms to respond creatively to external shocks, because they know that bankruptcy will never take place: the worst thing that can happen is that the government nationalizes the company.

Social Justice
Covering the losses of inefficient parastatal enterprises diverts scarce resources from the natural function of a government to provide health, education, and basic infrastructure for the population. Also, in many instances the limited resources from taxpayers are used to prevent capital losses for the shareholders and the bankers of a firm instead of attending to the most pressing social needs. Finally, in the frenzy of expanding the parastatal sector, many new firms are bailed out or incorporated hastily, without a careful revision by congressional (parliamentary) authorities, in relative secrecy and without any consideration for the distributional consequences of the decisions.

Having said that except in the case of strategic industries, the process of modernization leaves very little room for an industrialization based on state-owned enterprises, the question remains if private firms can do better. A priori, there is no single direct answer to this question, simply because in spite of the institutional reforms that come with trade liberalization, progressive tax reforms, and better industrial regulation, there will still be circumstances in which privatization could make things worse. It is also true, however, that in some cases it is possible to have a regulatory framework within which private firms can contribute more effectively to economic welfare than can state-owned enterprises.

Therefore, according to the literature, the reasons for not privatizing lay primarily though not exclusively in the welfare costs of private monopolies; the reasons for privatizing have to do with the high monitoring costs and other information asymmetries between the public, politicians, and managers of state-owned firms, which lead to contradictory objectives, bureaucratic meddling, overly centralized decision making, inadequate capitalization, excessive personnel costs, and high labor turnover. In the end, the decision will depend on the formation of an adequate institutional framework within which private owners can assure that their managers operate the firm efficiently, and the authorities can be sure that the market works to allocate resources where their marginal benefit equals marginal cost.[6]

Empirical studies on the comparative performance of public and private firms in countries that had gone through the privatization process before Mexico are consistent with this line of reasoning. For example, in a more detailed study in which market structure, regulation, and other relevant market conditions are carefully taken into account, it has been found that when market power is significant *but there is room for a certain degree of competition*[7] (such as in the case of airlines, the sale and distribution of gas, long-distance telephone services, public utilities, etc.), private firms are considerably superior to public enterprises in productivity and profitability.[8]

However, the same studies also show that when there is market power, but also a strong tendency toward natural monopoly, no unequivocal evidence supports one type of ownership over another, and that the final decision on whether to privatize depends on the particular characteristics of each enterprise and industry. In fact, in spite of the advantages that one may find in principle from transferring enterprises to the private sector, the risks of making mistakes can offset all potential benefits. Therefore, as the sale takes place, one has to make sure that the newly transferred firms operate in a regulatory framework that is propitious to the efficient management of its resources and favorable to competition.

At this point it is important to stress the fact that all that has been said in this section deals with the economics of state intervention, without any reference to the political economy side of the role of the state. I mention this because it is important to bear in mind that powerful political arguments in favor of nationalization of a given firm or industry can sometimes take precedence over strictly economic considerations. For example, a firm or a group of private companies may hold such a strategic position in the economy that it is possible for them to disregard and even reject the constraints imposed by the established legal order. The decision to nationalize the oil industry in Mexico, for example, entailed the need to restore respect for the Mexican Constitution and the rulings of the Supreme Court.

2.2 Microeconomic Considerations for a Privatization Program

The process of privatization[9] does not begin and end with the sale of a public entity. Attention must also be paid to the economic principles involved in the way in which the sale is made and how the enterprise will operate under private ownership. For example, there will be questions regarding the number of people to whom the enterprise will be sold (i.e., if the sale will be through private placements or public auctions), the nature of the transfer (if the enterprise is to be liquidated, merged, or broken up, or if the sale will mean the transfer of a regulated monopoly or the development of franchises), and the characteristics of competition and regulation after the sale. In general, there are two main microeconomic considerations in each case. First, the sale scheme must allow new private owners to control the firm's management effectively. Second, whenever possible, the firm must operate in a competitive environment, and if that is not possible, there must be an appropriate regulatory scheme to ensure internal and allocative efficiency. Some of the most relevant issues to examine are the following.

Guaranteeing Adequate Control for Shareholders
Both the law and the privatization process should provide a framework in which monitoring activities can be effectively centralized by a strong board of directors. It has been found that dispersed shareholding tends to lead to suboptimal monitoring of management for two reasons. First, an externality results when each small investor spends a great deal of resources monitoring the performance of the enterprise, and the benefits of this effort are diluted among the

rest of the shareholders. Second, as a result of factors such as economies of scale in the acquisition of information, it could be more cost effective to have monitoring activities concentrated in a group of people, thereby avoiding the possible duplication of effort associated with multiple shareholding. A good alternative for the privatization of large firms, when the resources of many shareholders may be needed, is to have a combination of a strong board of directors that will have the motivation to oversee the enterprise, supported by large number of small shareholders.

It is essential to advance in the development of the capital markets and the supporting regulation to make takeovers possible, openly and without introducing undesired financial instability. It is generally accepted that takeovers help generate the incentives for good managerial performance. Unfortunately, in developing economies the culture and the institutions necessary to carry out this type of operation barely exist—a strong reason to use the privatization process to help local participants learn more about corporate finance and these kinds of operations and develop a local capital market. Thus, whenever possible it would be advisable to use the stock market to carry out privatization operations. In addition, this is a good reason to start introducing new regulations on takeovers and holding companies to avoid the problems experienced in other countries.[10]

The mechanism of bankruptcy has to work properly. This may sound obvious in economies with a long market experience. However, large private enterprises were commonly bailed out by the Mexican government in times of crisis. As has already been mentioned, for all practical purposes the risk of going bankrupt had no effect on the prudence of business managers. Privatization is then insufficient if it simply means the reestablishment of the status quo, only to be followed by nationalization.

Employee shareholding schemes can have a favorable impact on internal efficiency. The participation of workers can be desirable because employees have more information than the general public on the amount of inefficiency that might be corrected. One of the problems with state-owned enterprises is that they lack the mechanisms to provide an incentive to workers to maximize long-run profitability. Workers' participation in the capital of the firm would strengthen their commitment for increased efficiency.

Creating a Competitive Environment[11]

Mergers—or for that matter, all kinds of measures that would permit the new private firm to hold or gain market power—should only be permitted when there are such economies of scale that entry leads to undesirable duplication of fixed costs. Then, unless the trade-off between allocative efficiency and economies of scale goes clearly in the direction of monopolies, mergers leading to gains in market control should be limited.

As happens with the rest of the elements of the structural reform policy, contestability and dismantling of barriers to entry are closely related and can support each other when adequately coordinated. For example, it is important to be sure that simultaneously to the privatization process, exogenous barriers to competition (such as tariff and nontariff barriers in the case of international competition) are eliminated, and that there is a comprehensive antitrust regulation aimed at curbing strategic deterrence practices on the side of the new private incumbents, such as limit pricing, preemptive patenting, etc.[12]

The design of the sale strategy can have a significant impact on market structure. Many of the regulatory problems that emerge with the transfer of public sector monopolies to the private sector can be solved in the design phase of the privatization scheme. A good example of this is the option of franchising (competition for monopoly),[13] where private operators may have the opportunity to outbid and displace public suppliers, especially in cases in which the product or service has simple specifications. Another example would be the decision to partition a public sector monopoly and sell its parts, versus the alternative of selling the monopoly as is and then proceeding to regulate, as typified by the telecommunications sectors, where it is possible to separate local telephone services from long-distance services.

2.3 Macroeconomic Considerations for a Privatization Program

From the macroeconomic point of view, it also has to be true that when there are complete and efficient credit and asset markets, the sale of public sector enterprises should not have any macroeconomic impact. In fact, what privatization means in the end is simply a change in the composition of the portfolios of the public and private sectors, without any change in their net positions. In consequence, if the price paid for an enterprise is equal to the present value of the stream of future profits discounted at an equilibrium rate of interest, a full Ricardian equivalence should apply, and neither interest rates nor consumption and investment paths, inflation, the current account, and the real exchange rate would be affected. In reality, the fact that markets are not perfect implies that this kind of neutrality will not necessarily follow. For example, if domestic financial markets are not fully integrated with the international loanable funds markets, it will certainly matter if the buyers borrowed abroad or are repatriating their own savings to make the purchase. For budgetary planning considerations, it will also be very important to distinguish between short-term and permanent effects of these kinds of operations. The most important relationships to look at when deciding on how the privatization program should form part of overall macroeconomic policy design are the following.

Real Sector Impacts
The sale of a public sector entity has two components: revenues from the operation itself, and the disappearence of all future flows of revenues or transfers between the government and the company. To ensure neutrality, temporary revenues should be used only to finance temporary spending in the same amount, or permanent spending in an equivalent amount in present value. For instance, if the proceeds from privatization are used to cancel outstanding public debt, it is only the savings that come from paying less interest that can be used to finance a permanent increase in current spending. Also, the reduction in net transfers to money-losing parastatal firms can be used to increase current spending on a permanent basis, while still assuring macroeconomic neutrality. If, on the contrary, the temporary revenues are used to increase permanent spending by the same amount, the net effect will be expansionary.

When domestic and foreign loanable funds markets are segmented, if the sale is made to foreign investors the operation will be neutral *only if* the price they pay is equal in present value to the remittances abroad in the future. This is not the case if there is any crowding in of additional foreign investment, which may happen if the decision to privatize is perceived as a move in the direction of a more favorable environment for business.

Another possibility is the crowding in of domestic investment. In this case, the privatization of public enterprises is again not neutral. The effects of privatization would then be expansionary. In addition, provided that firms have access to international credit markets to finance the external component of the crowded-in investment, privatization could also reinforce other macroeconomic policies targeted toward inflation and nominal exchange rate stability.

Monetary Effects
If the purchase is leveraged with domestic financing, the sale will be equivalent, from the standpoint of the money market, to an open market operation in which agents exchange liquid assets (such as deposits or short-term monetary instruments) for shares. This may have contractionary effects, at least for a while (i.e., until the reduction in the credit aggregates translates into less inflation). In this case, neutrality would call for an expansionary monetary policy.

If the purchase is leveraged with foreign financing or capital repatriation, and the inflows that usually begin to take place several months before the actual operation is completed are not sterilized, the result will be a (perhaps undesired) expansion of the monetary aggregates. Neutrality would then require contractionary monetary measures during this phase of expansion.

3 Privatization in Mexico

Starting from the consideration of its the macro- and micro-economic impacts as mentioned above, the privatization of public sector enterprises rests on three elements. The first is the legal framework, the second is a procedure that is to be simple, open, and nondiscriminatory, and the third a set of principles that are followed to apply that law to concrete cases. The first two elements can be found in written laws and decrees, while the third reflects more the administrative style of the authorities.

In this section we will briefly look at these three elements, and then proceed to review some specific cases such as the privatization of Teléfonos de México and the sale of commercial banks, to get a clearer idea of how the task has been carried out. In each it will be possible to identify the way in which the microeconomic considerations mentioned above have been taken into account in designing the sales strategy and setting up the regulation prevailing afterward. This section finishes with some tables that summarize the results achieved and the macroeconomic impact of the divestiture process.

3.1 A Framework for Privatization

3.1.1 The Legal Framework

The legal foundations for the divestiture process are clearly outlined in three articles of the Constitution of the United Mexican States. Article 25 establishes the limits to private sector participation and therefore the limits of the privatization program. It states that "The public sector will be exclusively in charge of the strategic areas listed in article 28 paragraph 4 of the Constitution, with the Federal Goverment as the owner and authority in charge of the entities created to that effect." These strategic activities are the minting of coins, the postal service, telegraphs, radiotelegraphs and satellite communication, printing of money, oil and all hydrocarbons, the basic petrochemical industry, radioactive minerals, and the generation of nuclear power, electricity, and railways. For all other activities it is therefore not only possible but consistent with the spirit of the Constitution[14] to seek the participation of the private sector through, among other options, privatization.

While these first two articles refer to what can be sold, Article 134 refers to the minimum conditions that have to be satisfied in the divestiture processes. For instance, paragraph 2 states that transfer of control of a parastatal enterprise to private hands "will be adjudicated through public auctions convened by public edict, so that participants can freely present their postures in a closed envelope, which will be opened publicly, to assure that the State gets the best conditions in terms of price, opportunity and other applicable conditions."

Other secondary laws complement the basic constitutional framework regarding divestiture operations different from sales. The Organic Law of the Federal Public Administration defines how parastatal firms can be declared bankrupt and liquidated, while the Federal Law of Parastatal Entities establishes the legal procedures for mergers and transfers.

Finally, when a public sector entity was created by law or decree of Congress, congressional authorization must be sought for the entity to be divested. Also to the extent that these operations may have an impact on the budget, in compliance with the constitutional obligation of the executive branch to inform the house of representatives on the financial state of the nation, there is also the obligation to keep it informed about the evolution of the divestiture process (Article 74).

3.1.2 The Sales Procedure

Each of the hundreds of parastatal firms sold goes through a process of twelve steps. This procedure has been designed to keep discretion to a minimum, to keep the procedure as clear and simple as possible, and to strictly observe all legal requirements. It can be briefly described as follows:

Step 1. Divestiture proposal by the ministry responsible for the firm   The process gets formally started when the ministry responsible for the firm to be divested (legally referred to as the sectorial coordinator) presents a divestiture proposal to an interministerial commission formed by the heads of the ministry of finance, the general comptroller of the United Mexican States, the ministry of commerce and industrial promotion, the ministry of labor, and the central bank (Spanish acronym: CIGF). This proposal must explicitly establish that the firm is neither strategic nor classified as "high priority" in the Constitution. For example, if one is talking of a hotel, the proposal will be presented by the ministry of tourism; that of a sugar mill will be presented by the ministry of agriculture and hydraulic resources.

Step 2. Resolution by the interministerial commission   The CIGF analyzes the proposal and, considering the general situation of the entity, its area of activity and its operational history, decides on the most adequate divestiture alternative. This could be liquidation, closing, merging, transfer, or sale.

Step 3. Agreement to start the sales process   If it has been decided that the best option is to sell the enterprise, in accordance with the law, the firm is placed under the sole responsibility of the ministry of finance, which is authorized to carry out the sales process.

Step 4. Appointment of the sales agent   The ministry of finance in all cases chooses one of the eighteen commercial banks in the country as sales agent. The decision on the bank chosen is made considering its experience and work load. The office of privatization at the ministry of finance studies the situation of each firm, and in close collaboration with its agent, designs the sales strategy.

Step 5. Sales guidelines   Once the sale strategy has been designed, the agent presents concrete guidelines on notifications to the public, rules for the sale, timetables for visits, delivery of prospects and business profiles, size of the deposits, etc. The entire package has to have the final approval of the office of privatization.

Step 6. Profile and prospectus   The agent prepares two documents: the *profile,* which is a short document that includes a general overview of the enterprise, and simultaneously publishes in all major newspapers a public notice informing all interested parties that the firm is on sale and that preliminary information is available. The second document is a *descriptive prospectus* that contains detailed information on financial, commercial, technical, and labor issues.

   In most cases, to be eligible to receive a prospectus, a deposit, whose amount varies depending on the size of the business in question, is required. A letter must also be signed stipulating that the information contained in the prospectus may not be released for a certain time. In addition, interested buyers can make as many technical visits to the establishment as they consider necessary, and all questions will be answered in writing and shared with the other bidders.

Step 7. Technical and financial appraisal   On the basis of all available information, the agent completes a technical and financial appraisal to determine, using a variety of methods,[15] a minimum reference price. In most cases this appraisal is made by Mexican financial experts, but sometimes, due to the nature of the firm, there is additional support from international advisers. Outside consultation was used in determining the prices of Mexicana Airlines, Teléfonos de México, Cananea Mining Company, Sidermex, and Altos Hornos de México and the commercial banks.

Of the sales completed during the administration of President Salinas, 89 percent of enterprises (representing more than 98 percent of total value) have been sold at a price equal to or higher than the reference price, and only 11 percent of the firms, representing 2 percent of the value were sold at less than the reference price. Most of the latter were sugar mills, mainly because of the uncertainty prevailing in the sugar markets and the precarious physical condition of plant and equipment.

Step 8. Evaluation of received offers   According to the sales guidelines issued by the agent, on a specified date all offers are received in sealed envelopes. This event takes place openly before a notary public and in the presence of representatives of the ministry of finance and the general comptroller. Immediately afterward, the bank in charge of the sale proceeds to homologate the offers to make them comparable. For example, the agent not only looks at the price in the offer, but also considers the plans that the potential owner has with respect to the future of the firm, even though the price is still the dominant criterion.

Having done this, the agent prepares a recommendation to the ministry of finance on the proposal that represents the best alternative. If all offers are below the reference price, or if there is only one offer, the CIGF may decide to assign the firm to one of the participants or to start the sale process over again. In most cases, there are no more than three auction rounds. If the sale cannot still be made, the CIGF proceeds to negotiate directly with the participants under the supervision of the general comptroller.

Step 9. Resolution and legal authorization for the closing of the sale   When the CIGF gives a favorable resolution for the sale of the company, the ministry of finance releases an official authorization for the sale in favor of the participant who presented the best proposal.

Step 10. Signing the sales contract   The deal is closed with the signing of a contract and payment is made to the treasury. At this point, the ministry of finance completes an audit of the sale, and if there are any claims, the corresponding reimbursements are made at once.

Step 11. Divestiture   The ministry of finance sends a notification and a copy of the sales contract to the ministry of planning and budget to comply with all legal formalities to officially declare the enterprise out of the parastatal sector.

Step 12. Preparation of the "white book"   When the sales process has concluded, the agent has the obligation to prepare the so-called white book, which includes all documents relevant to each stage in the privatization process. The head of the office of privatization sends it to the ministry of finance and to the general comptroller. Additionally, a copy is sent to the accounting commission at the house of representatives, which can make all the observations and studies it may deem necessary.

3.1.3 Some Practical Principles on Privatization

In addition to respecting laws and procedures, the characteristics of the Mexican privatization program have been marked by the administrative style in which the laws and the procedures are applied. More than legal or economic concerns, these principles respond to political economy considerations, such as the nature of the entrepreneurial class, respect for the democratic right of society to be informed, and the experience from which one starts and carries on through the process. In what follows, I would like to suggest a list of eleven practical principles derived from everyday practice, which although not necessarily required by law, have become useful guidelines for the authorities during the process.

1. *First, privatize the private sector.* Privatization is not simply the transfer of state-owned enterprises to private hands, but a much more comprehensive concept of reform that implies the redefinition of the role of the state and of civil society in the production and distribution of income. In the new context of increased market competition and private ownership, there is no room for direct subsidies to production and other distortions that work against the development of efficient enterprises. Therefore, before the sale of firms can begin, one must be sure that the new owners face realistic market conditions by implementing measures such as the correction of public sector prices—i.e., by setting them at cost-recovery levels while not exceeding relevant international references—and the opening up of the economy.

2. *Start with small firms and work up as fast as possible.* There are several reasons to be prudent about the sequence of privatization. We bureaucrats do not necessarily know how to sell. We have to accept that learning all the technicalities

of privatization take as much time as any other complicated task of public policy. Second, it is important to minimize risks. If one makes a mistake selling a nightclub or a bicycle factory, that is too bad, but it is not as tragic as if these mistakes are made in the sale of the largest commercial bank in the country, the telephone company, or a major airline. Besides, the authorities will need time to explain the macroeconomic and income distribution advantages of the divestiture policy, particularly when the official view for the last fifty years had been that more state presence is a precondition for more social justice. This political task of education and persuasion is based on the argument that resources freed from divesting inefficient firms will be destined for education, infrastructure, and health programs, such as has been done in President Salinas's National Solidarity Program.

All this does not mean that the process has to come along slowly. On the contrary, as with all other elements of the stabilization and structural change strategy, it is important to go as fast as possible. The basic message here is that it is important to acknowledge that sequencing of privatization is important, and that in spite of all efforts it will inevitably take some time.

3. Privatization cannot succeed without macroeconomic stability. Progress in the areas of macroeconomic adjustment, deregulation, and structural change is an essential foundation for a successful privatization strategy. Only in an environment of economic certainty and confidence can people genuinely think about productive investment and consequently offer a higher price for public sector firms. Let me provide an example. One week before Mexico signed an agreement with the commercial banks renegotiating its external debt, we had not received a single offer above the reference price for Mexicana Airlines. One week after the deal, the office of privatization had received seven offers, four of them well above the minimum price.

4. *Sometimes one bankruptcy is worth many sales.* Not all public sector enterprises can be sold. Many of them are not viable. Acknowledging this is an essential step, and maybe one of the most difficult hurdles to overcome, because there will be many who think that the goal of the stabilization program is to save it all. On many occasions it will be preferable to give, once and for all, generous severance payments to workers than to continue draining public finances forever. Besides, bankruptcies constitute a clear signal to society that the government knows what it is doing and that it is committed to doing whatever is necessary to permanently correct the economic disequilibria.

5. *Keep the process under control.* Experience has shown that centralized control of the privatization operations not only facilitates accountability, but also expedites the decision-making process. Centralization means having a single office responsible for presiding over the board of the firm on sale, appointing the general manager, and supervising all legal requirements of each divestiture alternative. This office can also play an important role in promoting new sales by encouraging potential buyers to participate, based on the record of previous successes and experiences.

6. *It can prove advantageous to restructure large public sector firms and companies in strategic sectors, before privatization.* In addition to the tasks that the office of privatization has to accomplish in every situation, there are cases in which the enterprise has had to be administratively and financially overhauled before it could be sold. The leverage of the authorities is often required, such as in the rewriting of the labor contract and personnel layoffs, financial restructuring

operations that need legal changes, or the design of franchise agreements. Here it is important to remark that the office of privatization would conduct only major managerial changes, whereas the executives of the firm would have to play a primary role in all those processes specific to the business operation in the areas of their expertise.

7. Sell on a cash basis. This is a basic principle closely related to the idea that privatization is an irreversible process that transfers the possession of assets from the government to the private sector on a once-and-for-all basis, and is also aimed at breaking the pattern of industrialization based in an overly protected and inefficient capitalist sector that would look at the government as a safety net in case of bankruptcies. Selling on a cash basis is a way of cutting the umbilical cord between the government and new firms. It also assures that the firm will not go back into government hands or the unpaid balance used for blackmailing the government.

8. Use creative financing. There is no single way of selling the stock of a firm. Multiple ideas of financial engineering can be developed in the context of existing institutions and regulations, and it is important to see how they can be used to facilitate and improve the conditions of each transaction. For instance, part of the stock could be placed on the local stock market; part on the international financial markets, or through private placements; or one could design mechanisms for the participation of workers, to further the interest of foreign investors, and so on.

9. Keep the public informed. To gain credibility in the divestiture process, it does not suffice to do things according to the law; people have to know that things are actually done honestly. This is a powerful reason for having an active policy to keep people informed. For example, the announcement of the sale has to be made not only in the newspapers but also on TV and radio and in other mass media; one has also to describe the characteristics of the buyer and the form of payment. Last but not least, Congress and the general comptroller have to be briefed on a permanent basis.

10. When spending privatization revenues, be prudent. Once the sale is completed, one has to decide what is to be done with the transitory revenues of a sale to have a permanent impact on public finances. Prudence and common sense suggest that one-time revenues from privatization should not be used to finance current spending. If so, this source of government revenues will eventually disappear, leaving a large hole in public finances. In contrast, a sizable part must be devoted to reducing government outlays on a permanent basis by, for example, reduction in the stock of debt or, given extraordinary circumstances such as the instability of world financial and oil markets like in the Persian Gulf crisis, building up reserves to buffer the impact of wide fluctuations in public sector revenues. Reducing the debt opens new ways to increase permanently government expenditure in education and basic infrastructure.

11. Remember that divestiture leads to more effective government. The years of inflation, crisis, and adjustment helped us to realize the unacceptable high social costs of statism. If a country is really committed to its people, why then would its government own an airline and use billions of dollars of taxpayers' money to update its fleet when only 2 percent of its population has ever flown, and at the same time requires better public services. What would be the justification for keeping a steel conglomerate such as SIDERMEX, which in two decades accumulated losses of more than U.S. $10 billion through poor management, bad investment decisions, and severe productivity problems? As a simple matter of public policy and common sense, it is not possible to keep covering these losses when a fraction of this cost could have financed improved drinking water, sewerage, hospitals, and education to all the marginal communities in the southeastern part of the country. In contrast with what were considered the social grounds for a widespread participation of the government in the economy, examples like these show that the state reform through the divestiture of enterprises and the strengthening of social spending constitutes a truly progressive policy of distribution and development.

3.2 Two Concrete Cases

Although each privatization has its own special characteristics, two examples can help illustrate the range of decisions and the political and social considerations involved in every operation. The first is the sale of the national telephone monopoly (Telmex), and the second is the privatization of the commercial banks nationalized in September 1982.

3.2.1 The Privatization of Teléfonos de México
The privatization of Teléfonos de México started with an announcement by President Salinas de Gortari in March 1990 in the auditorium of the National Telephone Workers Union. At that particular time, and due to the strategic importance of the company, his message to the nation established that the operation should satisfy at least five basic criteria, over and above what was already stated in the law. First, there would be total respect for the rights of the workers, granting them the prerogative to participate as stockholders in the new company. Second, although

foreign investment would be allowed, Telmex should remain under the control of Mexican nationals. Third, the new owners would have to be committed to increasing the quality and coverage of service up to international standards. Fourth, sustained growth of the network had to be assured. And fifth, research and development had to be strengthened.

Immediately after this announcement, Telmex was put under the responsibility of the ministry of finance. The minister, as chairman of the board, appointed a new general manager, and together they started a comprehensive restructuring process, which included the following measures.

a. *Fiscal reform.* Telmex used to have a special tax regime consisting of a number of ad hoc duties, not necessarily linked to the operation or the overall performance of the company. The extremely burdensome tax structure was replaced by the general corporate tax regime.

b. *New labor contract.* A new labor arrangement was negotiated, consolidating the fifty-seven contracts in place (meaning that contracts were renegotiated on an average of once a week) into a single one. This gave the workers more job security while making future negotiations much more flexible.

c. *Debt renegotiation.* Telmex borrowed U.S. $220 million on international markets to "buy back" old debt, which was selling at almost a 70 percent discount in the secondary market. The bottom line was a net reduction in liabilities of U.S. $480 million.

d. *New fare structure.* The price structure was revised to eliminate the cross-subsidies from abnormally high prices for the long-distance service to local service.

To sell such a large enterprise without giving way to an unregulated monopoly, and to guarantee that the control of the firm would remain in the hands of Mexican nationals, it was necessary to follow a multitrack approach. With respect to regulation, the decision was made to create a new competitive environment in the industry. To do so, telephone services in the segments of cellular telecommunications and local telephone were immediately opened to competition. In addition Telmex, once privatized, had to operate under a franchise agreement that contemplates a five-year transition process conducive to the opening to competition of the long-distance services. During this time the company remains subject to a series of fare regulations as well as performance targets. For example, the agreement imposes minimum research and development and investment targets, so that installed capacity could grow at a rate of 16 percent during this first year and 20 percent the following four years. Explicit requirements were imposed regarding geographical distribution and type of service, and quality standards such as the complete digitalization of the network will have to be met.

The financial side of the sale has taken place in three stages. The first consisted of issuing a limited voting shares dividend, in such a way that each ordinary share would get 1.5 series "L." In this way, with only 20.4 percent of the capital it would be possible to control the entire firm. The first package of control shares was auctioned in December 1990, with three groups participating: the first one and winner was a consortium formed by Grupo Carso of Mexican businessmen, France Cable and Radio, and Southwestern Bell. The second group was formed by GTE of New York, Telefónica de España, and a Mexican group, and the third was another Mexican group. This phase was completed on 20 December 1991, with the exchange taking place at a price of U.S.$2.03 a share, the total operation being worth U.S.$1.7 billion. The labor union also participated in this step with the leveraged buy of 4.4 percent of the stock.

The second phase corresponded to the sale of half of the remaining control shares in the hands of the government (14.1 percent of the capital), this time through public place-ments in the financial markets of Mexico, the United States, Canada, Europe, and the Far East.[16] The second phase ended on 15 May 1991, with shares being placed at a price of U.S.$3.50 each. The third stage, to be completed at a later date, will consist of a final placement of the remaining government shares on international markets.

The overall sale and restructuring strategy made it pos-sible to complete the operation in very favorable terms. For instance, at the beginning of the present administration (1 December 1988), the value of Teléfonos de México calcu-lated from the price of its shares, as they were quoted on the New York Stock Exchange, was under $1.5 billion (U.S.$37 per share), whereas by 20 December 1990, Telmex would be worth more than $8 billion, and by mid-1991, this figure would well surpass the $13 billion mark.

3.2.2 The Privatization of Commercial Banks

Commercial banks are not like any other enterprise, simply because their role in the economy is not limited to the service they provide, but the way in which they operate can have a large impact on macroeconomic stability and long-term growth as suppliers of liquidity and intermedi-aries in the process of saving and investment. Therefore, the strategy of privatization to be followed will have to be different.

In the first place, the basic framework for the privatization of commercial banks had to be put in place by a careful definition of the operational and legal foundations for a modern and efficient banking system. As noted in chapter 2, in April 1989 the authorities initiated an important phase in the process of banking liberalization by the gradual elimination of the legal reserve requirement that was to end in September 1991. Of the same importance was the regulatory decision to allow banks to freely determine their borrowing and lending interest rates by year-end 1989. As a result of this, the market of banking services became increasingly competitive, which is an indispensable precondition for privatization. In addition to these changes it was necessary to amend the Constitution in May of that year, to allow for the private control of commercial banks. Immediately afterward the new Banking Institutions Act was enacted, together with the necessary regulations for the operation of financial groups.

Once the legal framework was ready, the privatization of commercial banks began, according to the rules set by a decree of President Salinas de Gortari on 5 September 1990. This decree created the Special Committee for Bank Privatization and established the following minimun conditions to be satisfied by every operation:

• Contribute to create a more competitive and efficient financial system.

• Guarantee a diversified participation in the capital of banks in order to foster investment in the banking sector and to preclude concentration.

• Adequately link the administrative capacities of the banks with their level of capitalization.

• Ensure control by Mexican nationals without excluding the participation of foreign investment.

• Promote the decentralization of banking operations and favor the regional development of the institutions.

• Obtain a fair price for the institutions, according to a valuation based on general, objective, and homogeneous criteria for all banks.

• Promote a balanced banking sector, as well as its operation under transparent and sound banking practices.

Looking at the international experience, it was found that governments follow essentially two different approaches regarding the sale of banks. One of them is that banks play such a strategic role in the economy that the highest bid price cannot be used as a criterion to assign it to an interested party: therefore the dominant criterion of selection will have to do with the seriousness and personal prestige of the candidates who wish to buy the institution. The second technique is that, provided that the mechanisms of bank supervision work reasonably well, there is no reason to worry about prestige and banks should be sold to the highest bidder.

In principle, there should be no reason to discard either of these points of view, for having a transparent standard to discriminate among parties gets rid of discretionality and reinforces the confidence in the divestiture process; while it is also true that banks have to be trusted to responsible entrepreneurs who have a reputation of knowledge and honesty in the financial sector. This is why, instead of choosing to follow one approach as opposed to the other, the privatization of Mexican banks used both.

Therefore, at the beginning of a privatization operation the role of the committee was to receive and register the applications of groups of entrepreneurs who were interested in buying a bank. These applications were then eval-

uated on the basis of probity and experience of the aspi-
rants, and only those who are considered suitable get the
right to participate in a second round. Here, all those groups
that get a registration are allowed to participate in the auctions for the banks, where the only prevailing criterion that
applies is the price, so the bank goes to the group that offers
the highest amount.

One closely related issue has to do with the valuation
technique, which is intended to be more complete and
detailed than in the standard cases, not only because some
of the banks are very big, but because it is acknowledged
that firms in the financial sector are affected differently by
changes in expectations and macroeconomic fundamentals
than the rest of the economy. In this way, before the committee determines what it considers an adequate reference
price, it looks carefully at three separate appraisal studies.
The first is a *financial appraisal* based on accounting information of the bank, and elaborated in accordance with strict
guidelines set up by the National Banking Commission; the
second is an *economic appraisal* prepared by an external con-
sultant that describes the business profile and presents
some opinions on the possible future performance of the
institution, based on individual and market trends; finally,
a third study prepared by the banks themselves looks at
their evolution and evaluates their market position and
business opportunities.

In addition to the two-stage sales policy, some other principles also influenced the style of bank privatization. For
instance, in compliance with the basic privatization criteria
of the presidential decree, sales have been implemented in
such a way that the structure of control combines a small
group of responsible and clearly identified shareholders
with a large number of small investors who can contribute

to strenghtening the capital base of the institution. That has been the case of BANAMEX (the largest commercial bank), whose holding company is made up of nearly 4,000 individuals who represent 80 percent of the capital; the remaining 20 percent is in the hands of nearly 1,200 regional firms.

Moreover, to the extent that one of the main ingredients of what makes retail banking efficient and effective in bringing the opportunity for economic progress to all parts of the country is its proximity to the needs of a particular region, the sale strategy was not limited to waiting for clients to come and buy the bank, but relied on a promotion effort from the authorities to reach successful local businesspeople. The outcome has been very encouraging: more than half of the banks have gone to regional groups, while those institutions with national coverage have taken the commitment to form regional boards of shareholders to gain a better understanding of the specific needs of their clients. For example, in the cases of BANAMEX and BANCOMER, a large number of businesspeople from different parts of the country got together and set up regional trust funds through which they bought an important portion of the capital of the banks and with that, the right to have an impact on the business strategy of the institution. In fact, the participation of these regional funds corresponds to 20 percent of the capital (with more than 4,000 entrepreneurs participating) in the former, and 25 percent (1,200 participants) in the latter. Moreover, summing up the eight banks that have been privatized, at present the number of individual investors involved is near 30,000.

In terms of the sales conditions, the bank privatization program has been very successful. During the first ten months, eight out of the eighteen institutions were sold for approximately U.S. $7 billion. With respect to the total capital of the banking system, these banks represent more than 64 percent. Between January and February 1992, the number of banks sold will reach twelve, accounting for 84 percent of total capital. The prices paid for these institutions in the auctions have not only been representative of the actual financial conditions of the institutions, but have also surpassed the expectations of the external advisors to the committee. The results are also very favorable when compared with international experience (see tables 4.3 and 4.4).

3.3 The Privatization Program in Numbers

The privatization of parastatal firms started almost nine years ago with the divestiture of many small firms. It was not until the administration of President Salinas de Gortari that the government took over the larger and more complicated cases (see figure 4.1). Between 1982 and 1988, a total of 905 enterpises were divested, out of which 204 were sold and the rest were either liquidated, merged, or transferred. In spite of the large number of operations, they amounted to a cumulative value of less than U.S. $500 million. However, they undeniably provided an invaluable

Table 4.3
Price obtained for commercial banks

	Times net income	Times book value
Mexico	14.6	2.8
U.S. and Europe	14.0	2.2

Source: Undersecretariat of Finance, Ministry of Finance, and CS First Boston.

Table 4.4
Revenues from the privatization of commercial banks

Bank	Date	Total ($U.S. million)
Mercantil	07 June 1991	202.9
Banpaís	14 June 1991	180.9
Banca Cremi	21 June 1991	248.1
Banca Confía	02 August 1991	294.1
De Oriente	09 August 1991	73.5
Bancreser	16 August 1991	139.8
Banamex	23 August 1991	3,190.4
Bancomer	27 October 1991	2,527.7
Total		6,857.4

Source: Undersecretariat of Finance, Ministry of Finance.

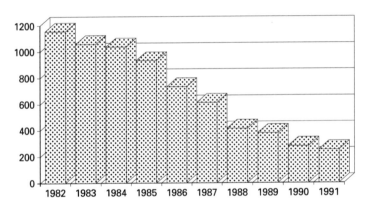

Figure 4.1
Number of parastatal firms (1982–1991)
Source: Office for Privatization. Ministry of Finance.

experience for the sale of much larger enterprises that began in 1989 (see table 4.5).

In fact, over the last three years the administration has finalized 310 divestitures of public enterprises that the Constitution does not consider strategic, from which it has received about U.S. $14.5 billion, such as Aeroméxico and Mexicana Airlines, Compañía Minera de Cananea (one of the largest copper mines in the world), SIDERMEX (the most important steel conglomerate in Mexico), and Teléfonos de México, and it is expected to finish the sale of commercial banks by mid-1992.

As a result, the parastatal sector has steadily reduced its importance in terms of total employment and production. In 1989, the last year for which there is revised information available on the GDP of the public sector, the participation of state-owned enterprises on total production had gone down from a high of nearly 25 percent in 1983 to less than

Table 4.5
Divestiture process of the parastatal sector

	Dec. 1, 1982– Nov. 30, 1988	Dec. 1, 1988– Nov. 1, 1991	Total
Concluded	595	310	905
Liquidated or closed	294	137	431
Merged	72	10	82
Transferred	25	7	32
Sold	204	156	360
In process			87
Parastatal sector in 1982			1,155
Parastatal sector in 1991			239

Source: Office for Privatization, Ministry of Finance, and SPP. The figure on the size of the parastatal sector in 1991 includes the effect of the creation of new parastatal entities.

16 percent. This figure is likely to be much lower now given that banking services alone account for nearly 2 percent of GDP (see figure 4.2). In employment terms, the number of people working in divested companies is slightly more than 200,000, which represented about 20 percent of the total employment in the parastatal sector in 1983 (and nearly 10 percent of total employment in the economy). This figure could reach 250,000 as the process of privatization nears its completion in 1992 (see table 4.6).

Regarding the macroeconomic effects, there are at least three aspects worth mentioning. The first has to do with the permanent effects of the privatization revenues. As was discussed in a previous section, the one-time proceedings from the sale of public sector enterprises should not be used to finance permanent increases in current spending on a one-to-one basis, simply because those revenues will not be recurrent. But if used to reduce the stock of debt, the savings in real interest payments that will occur year after

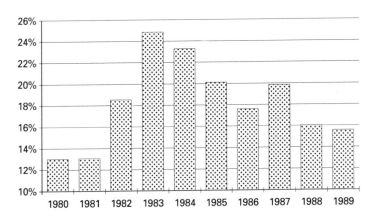

Figure 4.2
GDP of the parastatal sector/GDP
Source: Producto Interno Bruto del Sector Público, INEGI.

Table 4.6
The ten sold parastatal companies with the most employees

	Number of employees
Teléfonos de México	51,126
Bancomer	37,041
Banamex	31,385
Mexicana de Aviación	13,027
Impulsora de la Cuenca de Papaloapan	3,617
Astilleros Unidos de Veracruz	2,988
Compañía Minera de Cananea	2,973
Compañía del Real del Monte y Pachuca	2,416
Dina Camiones	1,678
Tabamex	1,259

Source: Office for Privatization, Ministry of Finance.

year can definitely be used to increase spending without any negative macroeconomic impact (see table 4.7).

However, it would be short-sighted to think that the only purpose of privatization would be to get the money coming from the sale. In fact, there are other elements of the divestiture and restructuring of the parastatal sector that can have a large macroeconomic impact. For instance, a second component of the program of reform regarding parastatal firms is the reduction of transfers from the federal government to state-owned enterprises. As shown in table 4.8, total subsidies to parastatal firms have gone down from 12 percent of GDP in 1982 to around 2 percent at present, as a result of the divestiture of inefficient and nonstrategic and nonpriority parastatal enterprises and of the previously mentioned *privatization of the private sector*. The reason is that the deficit of many state-owned firms was the reflection of subsidies and privileges granted to private enterprises.

Table 4.7
Once and for all revenues from privatization

	Revenues from privatization/public sector revenues (%)	Revenues from privatization/GDP (%)
1985	0.02	0.01
1986	0.04	0.01
1987	0.31	0.10
1988	0.67	0.20
1989	0.59	0.19
1990	4.32	1.19
1991	14.4	3.83

Present value (December 1991) $18,016 million

Permanent fiscal saving equivalent to the "once and for all revenues" from privatization[1]	.0933% of GDP

Source: DGPH, Ministry of Finance.
1. Assuming a long-term growth rate of the economy of 4.5% and a real interest rate of 6%.

Therefore, the rationalization of the parastatal sector has not been limited to the sale or liquidation of firms, but has also meant taking the prices of the goods and services provided by viable strategic firms to their market-clearing levels.[17] This substantial element of public sector savings also frees additional resources for spending in areas that truly correspond to the state, such as productive infrastructure and social programs, without any unfavorable macroeconomic consequences.

A third element of macroeconomic policy linked to the sale operations is that nonrecurrent revenues can be used to face nonrecurrent adverse external conditions. Such was the case with the war in the Persian Gulf at the beginning

Table 4.8
Subsidies and transfers from the federal government to the parastatal sector (as a fraction of GDP)

1980	8.37
1981	9.46
1982	12.71
1983	8.89
1984	6.96
1985	5.11
1986	3.31
1987	5.94
1988	3.42
1989	3.09
1990	2.51

Source: Cuenta Pública, various issues.

of 1991. The uncertainty that this event placed on the evolution of international oil prices—and therefore on the budget outlook for Mexico—made the authorities decide to set aside the revenues from privatization from the regular accounting of the treasury and the reserves of the Banco de México, so that they could be used strictly in the case of an eventual collapse in oil exports, to make sure that the economic program would be able to continue without any major adjustment.

The contingency fund has two accounts, one in pesos and one in dollars, and it accumulated all proceeds accrued from December 1990. As a result, by the end of October the balance was 20 trillion pesos (U.S. $6.5 billion) and U.S. $466 million. At that point, President Salinas de Gortari, considering that the elements of uncertainty that had created a need for the fund were no longer there, instructed the ministry of finance to apply the balance in the peso

Table 4.9
Contingency fund (as of November 1991)

From the sale of:	$U.S. millions	Billion pesos
Banks	0.0	6,229.2
Telmex	451.3	13,286.2
Others	0.0	127.4
Interest accrued	14.8	506.8
Debt repayment	0.0	20,027.0

Source: Office of the Treasurer, Ministry of Finance.

account to the reduction of the outstanding domestic debt (see table 4.9).

4 Conclusions

The privatization of the productive sector is one of the most important elements of the reform of the state. More than the mere exchange of assets between the government and the private sector, it represents a broader participation of civil society in economic and social development. It is not by any means a sign of retreat of the state from its natural mandate; on the contrary, it has become stronger to meet the social needs of the people and to provide an environment of long-term macroeconomic stability. This policy, together with the deregulation of the economy, fiscal reform, financial reform, and the government's new social spending program, completes a picture of a more modern Mexico where there are better opportunities for all.

5

Prospects for the Mexican Economy: A Look at the "New Mechanism of Transmission"

Almost fourteen years ago, when I was a Ph.D. student at MIT, I wrote a thesis with a rather technical and perhaps unappealing title: *Essays on the Mechanisms of Transmission: The Case of Mexico*. At that time I was interested in seeing and better understanding the ways in which microeconomics affected macrovariables in a small, open economy. The results of that research showed that given the way financial institutions worked, the nature of competition among domestic producers, and the distortions prevailing in the external sector, the Mexican economy looked very vulnerable to external shocks. Furthermore, the prospects for a sustained expansion of aggregate production in the future were incompatible with that kind of microeconomic setting.

If I were to write my thesis again today, I have the feeling that the results would be substantially different. In fact, after almost two decades of macroeconomic instability, Mexico has certainly come a very long way in reshaping its development strategy. As we have seen in the previous chapters, during the last nine years, and particularly during the first half of President Salinas's administration, the government and people of Mexico have pursued a strong and comprehensive program of adjustment and structural change. Beyond the mere correction of monetary and fiscal disequilibria, many of the difficult structural obstacles that had inhibited growth have been addressed. Examples of this are the implementation of a social pact to correct price inertia, the elimination of nontariff barriers to trade, the modernization of the financial sector, a far-reaching divestiture of public sector enterprises, renegotiation of the external debt, deregulation of the economy, education and agricultural reforms, the release of new rules to promote foreign investment, a thorough fiscal reform, and a new program of social spending and social participation to fight poverty.

Within this framework, considerable success has already been attained. Annualized inflation, measured by the consumer price index, has declined from more than 500 percent in January 1988 to less than 19 percent during 1991. The economy is regaining growth as a result of the surge of private domestic and foreign investment. The primary balance of the public sector moved from a deficit of 7 percent to a surplus of 6 percent of GDP, which is the equivalent to almost three fully enforced Gramm-Rudman acts. Our trade structure has been greatly diversified, as manufactures now account for more than one half of total exports, while oil represents less than one third compared to 75 percent in 1982. Some sectors and industries have been modernized, and the Mexican economy has become considerably more competitive and export-oriented as we move toward a North American free trade agreement.

In this new economic environment, marked by new investment opportunities and ways of participation of civil society, some macroeconomic indicators have changed their meaning from what they conveyed when I was a student.

For instance, in the late 1970s, a sizable current account deficit was a cause for concern. Usually it was the result of an overheated economy, pushed by government spending and financed by increasing external borrowing. Nowadays a current account deficit of the same size, relative to GDP, means a strong expansion of private investment financed by capital repatriation or direct flows from foreign investment into the country. In other words, in the *old mechanism of transmission* the sequence of events went from declining productivity and rents to the overprotected private sector, to the need to use government spending to keep the economy moving, to external overborrowing, to inflation, debt overhang, and recession. In contrast, in the *new mechanism of transmission* the sequence goes from better business opportunities derived from both changes in expectations and improved "objective" economic conditions to higher private investment, simultaneously financed by capital repatriation and direct foreign flows and complemented by additional domestic savings, to an improvement in the standard of living of the population supported by growing productivity and the corresponding appreciation of the real exchange rate, without a loss of competitiveness—all in an environment of lower inflation and exchange rate stability (see table 5.1).

The purpose of this last chapter is to comment on the challenges and opportunities ahead, starting from the notion that *there is a lot yet to be done,* especially in terms of microeconomic efficiency and equal access to opportunities for everyone. Section 1 presents a simple model to illustrate the way in which the governmental actions behind the program of state reform are reflected in the balance of payments and financial markets, and how they compare with the performance of the economy ten years ago. Section 2

Table 5.1
Old and new mechanisms of transmission

Old	New
1. Few investment opportunities for private sector agents. Social pressures from rising unemployment.	1. Rising expectations and emergence of new investment opportunities from deregulation, privatization, and external trade.
2. Government spending to keep up demand, production, and employment. Lower spending on infrastructure and social services.	2. Fiscal and monetary discipline to open new spaces for private sector financing in an environment of price and exchange rate stability. Higher spending in infrastructure and social services.
3. The increase in aggregate spending, particularly *public sector investment*, translates into a trade deficit, as a large proportion of the components of new projects are imported.	3. The increase in aggregate spending, particularly *private investment*, translates into a trade deficit as a large proportion of the components of new projects are imported.
4. Due to an incomplete financial system and a tax system that already puts a very heavy burden on taxpayers, the government has to borrow abroad to fill the gap from higher spending.	4. The new investment is financed via capital repatriation and direct flows from foreign investors. There is also new financial savings as a result of a liberalized financial sector. The new public sector savings derived from the permanent effects of privatization and the fiscal reform also contribute to free financial resources for the expansion of the competitive sector.
5. During the phase of expansion there is a real exchange rate appreciation, which translates into additional current account disequilibria.	5. During the phase of expansion there is an appreciation of the real exchange rate, as people regain their standard of living. However, the relative increase in the price of nontradeable vs. tradeable goods reflects the increases in labor productivity and not a demand-driven overheated economy.
6. The process ends with the inability to keep borrowing abroad indefinitely. The collapse comes in the form of a massive devaluation, recession, and high inflation.	6. The expansion continues as inflation recedes to international levels, as a result of higher productivity and the confidence of producers, labor, and consumers. The exchange rate stabilizes, and any further appreciation of the real exchange rate is essentially a reflection of productivity differentials.

contains the concluding thoughts to these lectures. We will look at what we have learned from what has been achieved, as well as from our setbacks in the experience of stabilization and structural change. Finally, we will make a brief assessment of the challenges that Mexico must continue to face in the years ahead.

1 The Macroeconomic Effects of State Reform

1.1 The Stylized Facts

Although the process of macroeconomic adjustment and structural change involves practically all sectors of the economy and society, thereby affecting a large number of variables, one could make a strong case about the long-term effects of the state reform in Mexico by focusing on four key factors.

The first is the current account. Because Mexico is a labor-abundant, capital-scarce country, it is to be expected that it would be a net importer of capital. That was the case throughout the postwar years until 1983, when the country became a net exporter of capital. During the years of the *desarrollo estabilizador,* the current account deficit oscillated between 2 and 3 percent of GDP, and could be financed with prudent external borrowing and direct foreign investment. In the late 1970s and early 1980s these deficits were larger and essentially covered by government external borrowing, until no additional foreign credit could be obtained. During the phase of debt overhang, the country had to run large current account surpluses. This situation was reversed three years ago when the economy returned to what has to be the state of long-run *normality,* to become once again a net importer of capital (see figure 5.1).

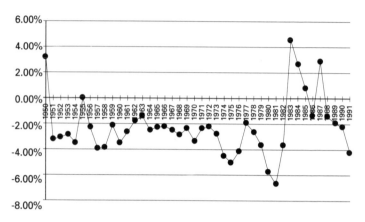

Figure 5.1
Current account balance/GDP
Source: Banco de México.
1) Value for 1991 is estimated.

A second variable is the fiscal balance. During the 1950s and 1960s, public finances were characterized by a very moderate deficit as a fraction of GDP. In contrast, the 1970s and 1980s were marked by a rising public sector deficit that coincided with the widening of the gap in the external accounts. The balance of payments collapse was much the result of the disequilibria in public finances. Since 1989 this strong correlation between the external gap and the public sector gap no longer applies. Now the external deficit increases in spite of the return to the long-run *normality* of a very small deficit or balanced budget (see figure 5.2).

The third piece necessary to complete the story of the transition is the behavior of private investment. In a first stage, as a result of the incentives put forward by the import substitution policies, private investment jumped from around 7 percent of GDP to nearly 13 percent. Those levels were maintained for practically twenty-five years, until the

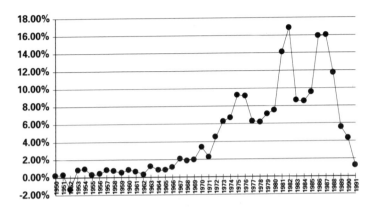

Figure 5.2
Public sector balance/GDP
Source: Elaborated with data from Banco de México.

1980s, when the flow of private capital formation dropped to its lowest levels since 1955. This contractionary process stopped around 1987, and since then investment has been rising at a much faster pace than GDP. This time the external gap, as shown by the current account deficit, is a response to the increase in private investment and not the deterioration of public finances (see figure 5.3).

The fourth variable, and in a sense the bottom line, is the accumulation of foreign reserves. In previous cases, the episodes of deterioration of the current account beyond their historical trends were accompanied by a significant loss of reserves. This time the increase in foreign investment and the repatriation of capital has not only compensated for the expansion in imports, it has also permitted the accumulation of significant amounts of foreign exchange. For instance, whereas on 1 November 1989, international reserves were $7.3 billion, one year later they reached $8.42

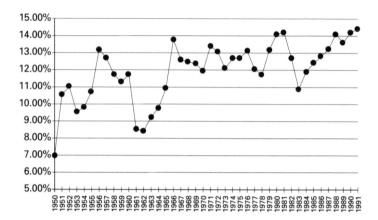

Figure 5.3
Private investment/GDP
Source: Elaborated with data from Banco de México.
1) The numbers for 1991 are estimated.

billion. Reserves doubled the following year, to reach $16.7 billion on 31 October 1991 (see figure 5.4).

1.2 A Simple Model

Some interesting details on the recent performance of the Mexican economy can be highlighted with the help of a simple system of one identity and four behavioral equations that relate investment, capital repatriation, and public finances. These basic relationships are:

a. The national accounts identity (savings = investment).

b. A function that explains the behavior of private domestic investment, depending on the degree of macroeconomic stability, the available financial savings, and the overall business environment as measured by the fiscal burden,

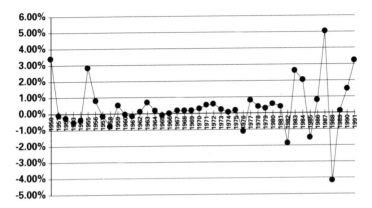

Figure 5.4
Accumulation of net foreign reserves/GDP
Source: Elaborated with data from Banco de México.

total government subsidies as a fraction of GDP, and the budget balance.

c. The level of financial savings as a function of domestic private savings and capital repatriation (private capital flows net of net foreign investment). The model assumes that direct foreign investment is financed one-to-one by financial flows from abroad.[1]

d. The flows of direct foreign investment, which depend on macroeconomic stability, the overall business environment as measured by the same proxies used for the domestic private investment function, the real exchange rate, and the situation of the world economy.

e. An equation for the flows of capital repatriation, which depend on the level of the real exchange rate and on the flows of private investment.

The economy described by these equations is in fact very similar to the most simple macroeconomic models of the

IS-LM type, but presented in such a way it highlights the connections between private investment and capital repatriation. In essence, the intention of the exercise is to study the change in these equations as a result of the structural transformation of the economy. To simplify the analysis, one could take the whole series of reforms listed in the previous four chapters and classify them into two groups. The first would include institutional changes such as financial liberalization, and the second would deal with the change in business opportunities. Although these do not mean per se a change in institutions, they certainly have the potential of inducing new investment and growth. Among these factors are *announcements of* an accord in principle to renegotiate the external debt, the prospect of a free trade agreement, or the government's intention to privatize the banks. This basic model tries to capture these two types of changes with two dummy variables, one that looks for a change in the slope and intercept of the equations after the liberalization of interest rates and during the fast process of financial innovation, and the other that breaks the sample by mid-1989, when the aforementioned news became known.

Comparing this model with the basic textbook, open economy, Keynesian model, the only variations included here are the specification of an equation of investment, which depends on the degree of financial savings, and a more detailed view of what determines international private capital flows.

The reason for including the first variation is to see another angle of the role of financial institutions in economic growth. But here, in contrast to what was done in chapter 4, the emphasis is placed on the investment side. It is to be expected that when the increase in financial deepening reflects new and more efficient institutions, investment opportunities that were not previously feasible because of the segmentation of markets will now take place. The reason for the second variation is to look at the different motivations for capital repatriation. For instance, it has been claimed that at some stage, capital outflows and reflows were not connected with the funds to be invested, but rather with financial speculation, and therefore no reflow could be considered permanent. What is to be tested, therefore, is if people are now bringing back their money (or obtaining credit abroad) to engage in productive activities therefore *automatically* financing the imports linked to that new investment.

The definitions and results from the estimation of this model are reflected in tables 5.2–5.6. To test for a structural break, one could start from a benchmark model that corresponds to the economy before these events took place, and then compare the results with what the economy looks like afterward. Drawing the results of tables 5.3 to 5.6, with a value of 0 for both dummies, what comes out is figure 5.5, which reveals some interesting characteristics of the Mexican economy before the process of structural change. Equation 1 is plotted in the upper left-hand side orthant, and shows that before the liberalization of interest rates, private investment was negatively related to the level of financial savings. The reason is that, in a context of segmented financial markets, the increase in financial savings is due mainly to the effects of the inflation tax[2] and not to financial mediation. This also means that firms that had relied on self-financing to carry out their projects would see those resources pulled out to finance the government imbalances.

Equation 2 is shown in the lower left-hand side orthant. As is expected, financial deepening depends essentially on

Table 5.2

A simple model of private investment financing for the Mexican economy

Sample: monthly data from 1980.01 to 1991.04
Method: maximum likelihood

Definitions	
IP	Private investment/GDP. Using the index of private investment of the Banco de México. Monthly GDP interpolated with quarterly GDP from INEGI.
AFIN	Financial savings/GDP. Financial savings defined by the change in M4. Series prepared with information from the Banco de México.
INF	Annualized rate of inflation. Source: Banco de México.
SUBSI	Subsidies plus transfers of the federal government/ GDP. Source: DGPH, Ministry of Finance.
DEF	Public sector deficit/GDP. Source: DGPH, Ministry of Finance.
AIP	Domestic private savings/GDP. From the national accounts identity it was calculated as IP + DEF − RCP.
RCP	Capital repatriation/GDP. Defined as the private capital account of the balance of payments, minus direct foreign investment, plus errors and omissions, all divided by GDP. Source: Banco de México.
IE	Direct foreign investment/GDP. Source: Banco de México.
TCR	Real exchange rate, defined as nominal exchange rate times the external price level divided by the domestic price level. Index: 1970 = 100. Source: Banco de México.
MERC	Unemployment rate in the United States. Source: Bureau of Labor Statistics.
DUM1	Dummy variable, which is zero from 1980:01 to 1982:12 and 1 from 1983:01 onward.
DUM2	Dummy variable, which is zero from 1980:01 to 1989:05 and 1 since 1989:06 to 1991:04
CFIS	Tax revenues/GDP. Source: DGPH, Ministry of Finance.
CREC	Annual rate of GDP growth. Elaborated with information from the Banco de México and INEGI.

Table 5.3
Results of equation 1

Dependent variable: IP	Coefficient	t-Statistic
Constant	.046	4.32
AFIN	−0.24	−8.04
AFIN*DUM1	0.48	2.60
CREC	0.083	1.95
CFIS	−0.14	−1.99
SUBSI	0.019	0.08
DEF*DUM1	−0.19	−1.50
IP(−1)	0.67	−5.5
$R^2 = .85$		

Table 5.4
Results of equation 2

Dependent variable: AFIN	Coefficient	t-Statistic
Constant	−0.068	−4.65
AIP	.464	4.02
RCP	0.80	2.98
AFIN(−1)	0.42	2.01
$R^2 = .93$		

Table 5.5
Results of equation 3

Dependent variable: IE	Coefficient	t-Statistic
Constant	0.003	3.16
DUM2	0.001	1.43
INF	−0.001	−.042
CFIS	0.03	0.69
SUBSI	0.02	0.59
TCR	0.04	2.90
MERC	−0.01	−1.45
IE(−1)	0.45	9.50
$R^2 = .69$		

Table 5.6
Results of equation 4

Dependent variable: RCP	Coefficient	t-Statistic
Constant	.025	2.70
DUM2	−0.021	−1.29
IP	0.086	0.93
IP*DUM2	0.92	2.60
TCR	0.0005	3.10
DEF	−.176	−2.12
RCP(−1)	0.35	6.43
$R^2 = .81$		

the levels of domestic savings and also on capital repatriation. An interesting comment here is that the reflows of capital going directly to the financial system, in a context of financial repression, did not necessarily translate into investment. Instead they become part of a "speculative" portion of the firm's portfolio.

Combining equations 1 and 2 gives as a result the downward-sloping equation $I=I(RC)$ in the first orthant.[3] Finally, equation 4 shows that, in the benchmark model, the flows of capital repatriation and capital flight were mainly connected to financial speculation rather than investment decisions (the elasticity of capital repatriation to investment is insignificantly different from zero). Therefore, dollars would come back in response to a shrinking fiscal deficit or after a devaluation to perhaps deal with liquidity problems, but almost certainly not because there were much better investment opportunities. This structural system of equations in fact represents the *old mechanism of transmission*. The way in which it works can be seen in the comparative statics exercise of figures 5.6 and 5.7. For example, an increase in the budget deficit would crowd out investment and fuel capital flight.

If a simulation were made to show what would happen with an increase of one percentage point of GDP in the government deficit, the result would be a decline of investment in the same proportion; the amount of capital flight would increase, and only a partial financing of that deficit would come from domestic savings (40 percent). The bottom line is that, for every peso of extra deficit, 60 cents had to be financed with external borrowing. As has been said repeatedly, this situation ended up imposing a binding constraint on the outlook for the long-term growth of the economy.

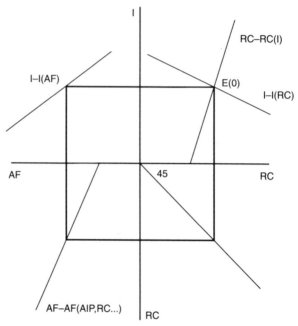

Figure 5.5
Benchmark model

The new mechanism of transmission is shown in figure 5.8. The position and slope of the curves now considers the effects of the structural break as implied by the coefficients of the dummy variables and of the interaction terms. These new coefficients reveal at least three important facts. First, after financial liberalization, investment became positively related to increases on that component of additional financial savings not related to the increases in the budget deficit. (The elasticity of investment to the budget deficit becomes significantly negative, at a 5 percent significance, after 1983.) This means that the advance in financial *deepening* resulting from the creation of new instruments is allowing

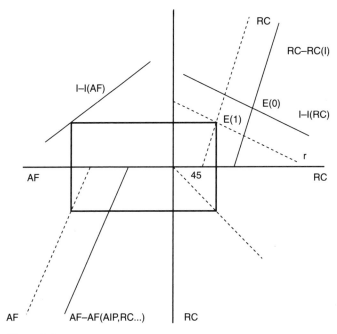

Figure 5.6
Effects of an increase in the fiscal deficit

firms to obtain increasingly more resources through the money and capital markets to implement viable projects.

A second observation is that private capital flows are now linked to real sector investment, and not only to financial speculation. This is established by the fact that the coefficient of investment in equation 4, which was insignificantly different from zero before the structural break of 1989, turns positive afterwards. This last result is maybe the most noticeable of the new mechanism of transmission because it shows that any increase in private investment is at least fully financed by capital repatriation (and/or additional for-

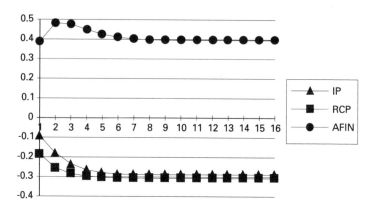

Figure 5.7
Effects of an increase in the budget deficit on one percentage point of GDP in the old mechanism of transmission (simulation)

eign borrowing), because the short-run coefficient is 1.08, and the long-run elasticity is 1.6. The difference translates into the accumulation of foreign reserves. In terms of figure 5.8, the effect of good news is shown by the increase in the investment elasticity of the private capital flows equation, and the "jump" in the level of autonomous private investment.

The exercise described in figure 5.8 corresponds to the effect of good news in the new mechanism of transmission. One example of this could be the announcement of the beginning of negotiations toward the North American free trade agreements which, even before anything changes in the objective business conditions, translates into new investment in those firms that want to get a head start once the formalities of the negotiation are concluded. In this way, the results of the estimated model illustrate how, in the past few months, the *prospect* of increased trade to the United States and Canada has fostered investment, which is auto-

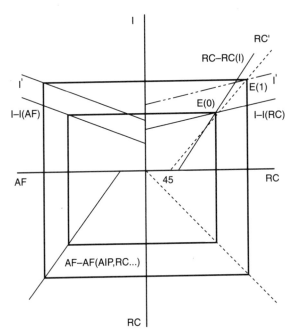

Figure 5.8
The new mechanism of transmission—effect of "good news" in the economy with liberalized financial markets

matically financed with private capital flows, and has allowed the exchange rate policy to remain consistent with lower inflation targets.

A third fact is that under the new institutional framework other increases in aggregate demand, such as a new expansion in the budget deficit, would have a softer negative impact on investment and external borrowing. This time an expansion of one percentage point of GDP in the deficit would be financed, in *equilibrium*, 60 percent with domestic resources and 40 percent with external borrowing (see figure 5.9). In summary, the model confirms what the stylized

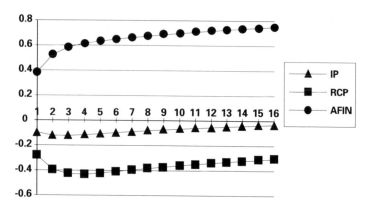

Figure 5.9
Simulation of a one-percentage point of GDP increase in the budget deficit, in the mechanism of transmission

facts had suggested: the Mexican economy looks and works very differently from the way it did ten years ago.

2 Economic Transformation and Long-Term Growth: The Challenges Ahead

Some time ago, Albert Hirschman[4] said that development was like a jigsaw puzzle, where it is easier to fit a particular piece the more neighboring pieces are already in place, whereas the hardest pieces to join are those with only one neighbor in place. This clever analogy evokes two very important economic principles that both academics and policy makers are rediscovering as we move from the decade of adjustment to a new time of reform and growth. The first is that at the beginning of the development experience—when an economy is no more than a collection of fragmented markets and regions—the setting up of government institutions, the construction of infrastructure, as well as the direct participation of the state in some areas of the economy, *is not only desirable but an indispensable precondition to starting the development process.*

The second principle is more in line with recent theories of endogenous economic growth.[5] It reflects the notion that the opening up of investment opportunities though changes in the environment where individuals work, save, and invest both creates and further reveals new investment opportunities. In Hirschman's example, once the difficult parts of the puzzle have been solved, it looks as if the following pieces begin to fall almost automatically into place. What this means for the role of the state in economic development is that after a period of protectionism and government intervention, it should be expected that growth would no longer respond as strongly to further involvement as it does at the very first stages of industrialization. Furthermore, this analogy conveys the notion that once the basic institutional framework is in place, it would be easier for civil society to find better ways to grow when their authorities—instead of participating directly in productive activities—are willing and able to open new business opportunities by means of deregulation, privatization, trade liberalization, and in general, by providing a favorable environment for competition.

Looking at the Mexican experience from the viewpoint of these two principles, one can gain a better insight into our background and put the nature and importance of all the changes of the last decade into perspective. For instance, in the years that followed the Mexican Revolution, and even by the years immediately after World War II, the country was very different from how it looks today. At that time the Mexican economy and society were geographically and economically fragmented and lacked the institutions necessary to link them in the enormous task of reconstruction and growth. However, our parents were able to envision the nature of the roles of state and civil society in a way that would make it possible to grow rapidly in an environment of price stability. In fact, it can be said that for some time the institutions behind the "old mechanism of transmission" *effectively served their purpose of creating an internal market,* of setting the basis for the emergence of an expanding middle class, and of providing the right conditions for the beginning of an industrial sector. In this way, between 1950 and 1970 Mexico was able to achieve what came to be known as the *economic miracle* of growing at an average rate of 6.6 percent with inflation of 4.5 percent (see figures 5.10 and 5.11).

The institutional changes behind the new mechanism of transmission are in turn the response of our generation to the challenge of development in a new economic context. In today's Mexico, the engine of our effort is the same nationalism that moved our parents, but this time it is the response to the risk of being left on the sidelines of the

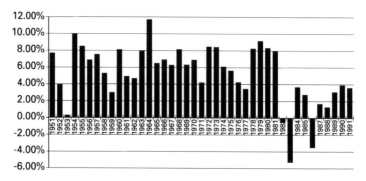

Figure 5.10
GDP annual rate of growth (1951–1991)
Source: Banco de México and INEGI.

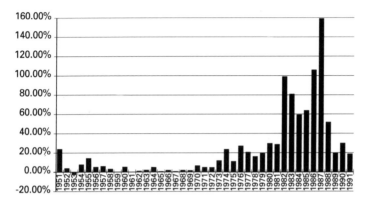

Figure 5.11
Annual rate of inflation (1951–1991)
Source: Banco de México.

world's new integration process. The example of other nations and our own experience has made us realize the enormous cost of seeking to avoid change and of looking only inward, while we are also witnessing the hope of building a new level of economic well-being. We as a country have come to the conclusion that it is not by closing our doors and trying to ignore what is happening abroad that we will ensure greater economic independence. Thus Mexico is looking after its essential interests when establishing new links with the rest of the world.

There are reasons to be optimistic about the future, because we know that we have been able to grow with stability in the past, and because the results achieved so far have showed us that the effort of adjustment and the trust among all sectors of Mexican society can actually be translated into economic and social progress. Whereas four years ago the country was heading for hyperinflation and recession, today inflation is down to the range of 20 percent per year, and the expansion in the levels of activity reflect the renewed confidence of Mexicans as well as foreigners in our capacity to respond to adverse circumstances.

However, there is still a long way to go. To bring inflation down to international levels and to assure that progress is sustained and fair, it is important to shift the emphasis away from short-term macroeconomic management to put the agenda for economic policy into the perspective of long-term development. Now, due to the adjustment efforts of the past, it is not only possible but necessary to implement measures to increase the rates of savings and investment in physical as well as human capital, to employ better technologies, to update our production organization method, and to make sure that poverty is eradicated. Therefore, there is no question that to respond to the challenge of our national project as stated in the Constitution, Mexico will have to continue the task of modernization for many years, with the same vigor as it has under the leadership of President Salinas de Gortari.

Looking at the fundamentals of economic growth, to produce more we will need to fully use the factors of production in the best possible way and to apply the best of human knowledge to make them perform better every time. The economic agenda for the next years will have to focus on the efforts needed to continue pursuing a profound microeconomic reform aimed at both economic efficiency and a better distribution of income and opportunities. The responsibility for carrying out such an agenda will have to fall on both public and private sectors. The government will remain obliged to provide better education, health services, and the implementation of a regulatory framework that guarantees the adequate functioning of markets. On the private sector side, firms and workers will have to implement with a great sense of urgency *true microeconomic pacts* to increase productivity and savings on a sustained basis.

To build up the Mexico envisioned by our Constitution, education will have to remain a major priority for action on the part of the government and society, to strengthen national integration, to be an instrument of justice by opening up opportunities where they do not exist, to preserve our cultural identity, and at the same time to provide the productive base with human capital with the skills needed to compete in the global economy. Here it is necessary to remember that expenditure in education, by increasing the stock of human capital of the least favored groups, creates permanent wealth, which by itself generates better job and income opportunities. The reorientation of public expenditure in this area increases social mobility and makes the present wealth and income concentration less permanent and more tolerable.

To support the investment necessary to grow and to create more jobs on a permanent basis, it will be necessary to increase the rate of domestic savings by means of mechanisms that make it possible for workers and the middle classes to save. In the future, the financial system has to get closer to the demands of the public, becoming an open, fair way to let people save toward a decent retirement, to deal with the enormous housing problem, and to make the business ideas of small and large enterprises a reality in every part of the country.

As demonstrated by the presidential initiative of November 1991, in the years to come we will have to work very hard to modernize the agricultural sector, devoting additional resources to building up its capital assets and creating options for production and partnership alternatives while respecting the integrity of the *ejidos*, communities, villages, and other types of rural settlements as they become more democratic and soundly based.

The strategic role of science and technology in the process of national modernization will become increasingly clear as Mexico completes the transition from instability to growth. To become and remain competitive in price and quality in the global economy, government and society will have to channel additional funds to promote basic and applied research, to stop the exodus of many of our scientists, and to develop the research capability of our industry.

Our industrial policy will also have to keep up with the new role of civil society in the economy. Once privatization is finished, the next step is to assure that the benefits of competition materialize through better resource allocation and income distribution. Advances in deregulation to reduce barriers to entry and an effective antitrust policy to ensure that everybody has the same opportunities to succeed in the marketplace are not simply a matter of economic efficiency, but of social justice.

The process of state reform will not be completed until no Mexican family lives below a level where all basic needs are satisfied. This means that the process of strengthening public finances by enforcing spending discipline and compliance with our tax obligations will have to continue being the backbone of our development strategy, to the extent that budgetary adjustment has made it possible to give attention to the most pressing demands of the population. Our generation has the commitment to work, to bring light to dark homes by supplying electricity, to address unsanitary conditions by installing drinking water and sewage systems, to install a caring attitude in health services, to correct public safety problems by providing street lighting and paving, and to offer justice.

The reform of the state has meant the transformation from a paternalistic government to an authority that governs for all without distinctions or exceptions, but which works the hardest for those who have the least. It has meant a government that will unfailingly insist on realistic measures, without forgetting how much is to be done, in loyalty to the nation.

From a historical perspective, Mexico has accomplished great feats in the course of its existence. Today, civil society and its democratically stronger and yet slimmer government are finding a new vitality and determination to make even greater progress with our sights firmly set on a better future.

Notes

Chapter 1

1. In Mexico the first open market operations for monetary regulation did not occur until 1978.

2. McKinnon (1973), McKinnon and Mathieson (1981), Fry (1988), and Lanyi and Scorogulu (1983).

3. Anaud and Van Wijnbergen (1988), Van Wijnbergen (1985), Hierro (1988), Deppler and Williamson (1987), and Dornbusch and Reynoso (1989).

4. We use the U.S. definition of billions = thousands of millions of dollars.

5. Eaton (1987), Ramírez (1985).

6. Díaz Alejandro (1981).

7. Krugman and Taylor (1978).

8. Van Winjbergen (1988), Reynoso (1990).

9. Taylor (1979), (1980); Fischer (1977), (1979), (1988).

10. Fry (1988), Fischer (1988).

11. Marglin (1984), Taylor (1983), Cardoso and Dornbush (1987).

12. Buira (1983).

13. Polak (1957).

14. Friedman (1968), Lucas (1973).

15. Taylor (1983).

16. Cardoso (1988), Modiano (1988).

17. Fanelli and Machinea (1988), Canavese and di Tella (1988).

18. Bruno and Fischer (1986); Bruno and Piterman (1988).

19. Spanish acronyms: PSE and PECE, respectively.

20. From here on, the following definitions are used:

Financial deficit = Deficit of the federal government + controlled parastatal sector deficit + uncontrolled parastatal sector deficit.

Primary deficit = financial deficit − total public sector interest payments (both internal and external).

Operational Deficit = total financial deficit − public sector financial mediation − official financial intermediaries' liabilities accepted by the federal government − the inflationary component of the nonfinancial public sector net internal debt in Mexican pesos plus the acceptance of liabilities by the official financial intermediaries of the federal government.

21. The real collection loss suffered by the government in times of high inflation due to the time taken to collect, between the moment they are accrued and the time they are actually received.

22. Dornbusch (1988).

23. Miller (1989).

24. See speech by Pedro Aspe, Minister of Planning and Budget, at the presentation of the Pact for Economic Solidarity, Los Pinos, December 15, 1987.

25. This result can be verified with the regression run on information from March 1988, taking as a dependent variable the shortage indexes of thirty-four products for which the Banco de México produces the relevant industrial data using the latest figures from the INEGI (Spanish acronym: National Institute for Statistics, Geography, and Information).

SHORTAGE =
10.37 − 7.7466 CONCENTRATION;
(4.220) (−1.79)
N = 34, R2 = .51; Method: WLS

SHORTAGE: Shortage index (expressed as a percentage). Source: Banco de México.

CONCENTRATION: Percentage of production belonging to the four largest companies of the corresponding industry. Source: INEGI.

26. The situation in which prices were too high *with respect to their equilibrium price* was more common in areas where there is a high degree of market concentration, and therefore where it is usually the case that problems of coordination could emerge. The following regression shows the relationship between the degree in which a price is above its *desired* level as predicted by a model, and industrial structure until August 1988 for the twenty-six categories in the consumer price index that correspond to industrial activities for which there is information on market structure and which are not under price control.

The dependent variable measures the percentage of *excess inflation* calculated as the difference between observed and simulated inflation for each sector using a model of inertial inflation. The independent variables are the degree of industrial concentration, the percentage of total consumption of each sector that produces basic consumer goods and the degree of liberalization, which is the percentage of production per branch subject to import permits.

ADELAN =
−.281 + .844 CONCEN − .154 PERMITS − 2.26 CONTROL;
(−14.1) (4.41)   (−0.61)   (−2.42)
N = 26, R2 = .99; METHOD: WLS.

ADELAN   Percentage of progress on prices (observed-simulated).

CONCEN   Industrial concentration index. Source: INEGI.

PERMITS   Percentage of industrial production subject to import price permits. Data from SECOFI.

CONTROL   Percentage consumption of the corresponding good subject to control or registration. Source: Banxico.

Chapter 2

1. For a comprehensive review of the theories of distribution and growth, see Marglin (1984). See also Aspe and Sigmund (1984).

2. Figure 2.1, elaborated with data from the World Bank, shows that there is a negative relation between growth and income distribution. The data for thirty-one developing countries for which there was information available on income distribution for the period 1965–1989 give a regression equation:

GROWTH =
3.915 − .0743*INEQ; R2 = .119;
CORR(GROWTH,INEQ) = −.3456.
(6.143)   (−2.017)

3. Alesina and Rodrik (1991), using a sample of twenty-four democracies for the period 1965–1985, estimated that a reduction of 10 percent in the income share of the richest 20 percent would raise the annual growth rate by about 0.3 percent.

4. Financial repression, as it is used in the related literature, refers to measures such as interest rate regulation, quantitative controls to credit, the use of obligatory reserves of commercial banks to provide credit to the government, etc.

5. Krugman and Taylor (1978).

6. Dornbusch and Reynoso (1989).

7. See Solís and Brothers (1970).

8. Table 2.1 was prepared with information from the Banco de México.

9. Multiple banks did not start operating until December 1976.

10. This reform gave place to a first review at the *encaje legal* regime. On April 1, 1977, the Banco de México established a single *encaje* rate for peso-denominated instruments for institutions constituted under the form of *multiple banks*.

11. Reynoso (1988).

12. Banks were allowed to receive dollar-denominated deposits, which were subject to a higher reserve requirement than the peso-

denominated deposits. This fact was provoked when currency substitution began to take place in anticipation of a maxi-devaluation, the worsening of the situation of credit rationing. See Dornbusch and Reynoso (1990).

13. Blanchard and Fischer (1989).

14. Feldstein and Horioka (1979) pointed out the interesting fact that if there were perfect capital mobility, it would not matter where savings were generated, but investment would take place whenever the marginal productivity of capital were larger. Therefore, if the savings rate in Mexico increased ceteris paribus the rest of the world, it would be expected that the external investment of Mexico in foreign countries would increase when the savings rate rises, and consequently the financial policies aimed at getting people to save more would contribute very little to investment and growth. The so called Feldstein-Horioka test looks at the relation between investment and savings, and it can be shown that the hypothesis of no-connection between savings and investment is rejected for the case of Mexico, being the coefficient for public investment insignificantly different from one at a 5 percent significance level.

Dependent variable: Gross fixed investment/GDP (1950–1990)
Method: Cochrane-Orcutt

Explanatory variable	Coefficient	t-Statistic
Constant	.108	3.57
Private savings	.539	3.86
Public savings	.805	4.58
Rho	.718	6.12

$R2 = .792$ DW = 1.70

15. The exercise refers to private voluntary savings defined as national income-direct taxes-social security contributions-inflation tax-consumption.

16. With series elaborated with data from the national accounts and the Banco de México, the following results were obtained using an instrumental variable method to take account of the possible problem of simultaneity between financial savings and private voluntary savings. The instruments used in addition to

the exogenous and lagged dependent variable were a dummy
variable after 1982, M4/GDP, the rate of external savings, the rate
of inflation, and the rate of financial savings lagged one period.

Dependent variable: Private voluntary savings/GDP (annual data,
1950–1990)

Method: Instrumental variables.

Explanatory variable	Coefficient	t-Statistic
Constant	−.00053	−0.17
Voluntary savings (T-1)	.50045	4.70
Direct taxes + social security/GDP	.04588	0.23
Financial savings defined as: Increase in M4/GDP	.27398	1.96
Income distribution defined as: wages national income	.14590	1.63
Real interest rate	.00085	2.26

$R2 = .89$ $DW = 2.05$

17. McKinnon (1973).

18. McKinnon (1973).

19. In this exercise it was taken as the ratio of labor income to total
national income.

20. For a more thorough discussion on the available data and the
evolution of income distribution in Mexico, see Aspe and Beristain
(1984).

21. Díaz Alejandro (1985).

22. Although in principle it may appear that a license and a concession are practically the same thing, there is a huge difference in
terms of the Mexican legislation. Concessions are given to carry
out activities that in principle correspond to the state; and they
are granted and removed, not only in terms of performance and
respect to the rules of the concession, but at the discretion of the
authorities. In contrast, a license is granted upon fulfillment of

certain nondiscretionary requirements, and is revoked only when the terms of the license are breached.

23. The industrialization experience of Italy in the 1970s provides an excellent case for small firms. By the end of World War II, Italy—as well as the rest of Western Europe—based its industries' reconstruction strategy on a wide-ranging array of subsidies and tax credits to strengthen large firms and promote investment in capital- and energy-intensive processes. In the late 1960s the largest Italian conglomerates began to face serious problems as a result of stronger labor unions and the inflexibility of capital-intensive activities in responding to sudden changes in costs and demand. In this context of a weakening industry, the oil shock hit Italy harder than any other industrial country. The response to the shock was twofold: the government put in place a broad program of industrial reconversion of large firms, while in the meantime new small enterprises appeared, headed mostly by workers who had lost their jobs during the crisis. As a result, a more flexible productive base replaced the large-scale chain-production methods, through small productive units that supply larger firms in those phases of the business cycle where demand is high, and that are able to produce finished goods during times of low aggregate demand. At present, firms with less than fifteen employees export around $30 billion a year, and account for near 50 percent of industrial output, in what is now the fifth largest Western industrial economy.

24. In Mexico the completion of one year of community service is a requirement for graduation.

25. The NGO assumes all risks and bears a cost of funding CETES plus a small spread, and finances the remaining needs for technical assistance.

26. The most important amendments to the tax laws took place in 1955, 1962, 1965, 1971, and 1972. For a more detailed description of each one of them, see Solís (1973).

27. See Gil (1984).

28. The fact that the personal income tax table had not been updated to take inflation into account, in addition to its original "regressive" design (see Kaldor 1973), implied that before 1979

collections were concentrated in the income bracket of one to five times the minimum wage. As the tax reform started to take hold, this bracket dropped from 58 percent of labor income tax collections to only 28 percent, while the highest bracket went up from a mere 8 percent to 25 percent.

Chapter 3

1. Under the program, the stock of foreign public debt grew rather conservatively between 1977 and 1980, with net flows averaging $3.2 billion, compared with more than $4 billion per year during the last three years of the previous administration.

2. Solís and Zedillo (1985).

3. Reynoso (1989) shows that having regulated or "incomplete" financial markets was responsible for the recycling of private external borrowing to capital flight, as well as for the explosive dynamics of both variables.

4. Except for credits granted or guaranteed by official entities.

5. Typically renegotiated to mature after eight years with four years of grace period. The mechanism was known as FICORCA.

6. Referred as MYRA or multiyear restructuring agreement.

7. Kindleberger (1971), Eichengreen and Portes (1986), Fishlow (1986).

8. This idea was presented under the name of debt-relief Laffer curve by Krugman (1989), and revisited later on by Sachs (1989) and Froot (1988), among others.

9. The total program resulted in a net $3.1 billion reduction of external public debt with commercial banks.

10. A more detailed and formal discussion of this issue was made at the time by Bulow and Rogoff (1989). See also the article by Luis Tellez in the *Wall Street Journal*, May 31, 1989.

11. Known also as Morgan bonds.

12. See, for example, Armendariz (1990), Eaton and Gersovitz (1981), Eaton, Gersovitz, and Stiglitz (1986), Sachs (1983), Krug-

man (1985), Corden and Dooley (1989), Dornbusch (1988), Bulow and Rogoff (1988), and Boreztein (1989), among many others.

13. Before the turning point of the debt-relief Laffer curve.

14. Extended fund facility.

15. $4,135 million for three years, to be extended for a fourth year at Mexico's request.

16. June 13, 1989.

17. MYRA plus all "new money" lent during 1987 and 1988.

18. Direct buybacks were not legally permitted by the previous debt agreements.

19. Mexico's export-import bank.

20. Eurobonds that can be converted at the investor's option into equity.

21. Nominal protection defined as (international prices/domestic prices) $-$ 1.

22. See Tenkate (1990).

23. Input-output matrix, the capital coefficients matrix, and the structure of protection (average) of 1985.

24. 1986 is excluded from this calculation to set aside the effects of the massive deterioration in terms of trade experienced in that year.

25. Baldwin (1989), for example.

26. Porter (1990), Whalley (1989).

27. Krueger (1978), for example.

28. As well as the formation of human capital and the modernization of the agrarian legislation.

29. The notation is the same as used for programming in GAMS205. Concretely, in this case a product of two matrices $(A(I,J)*B(I,J)$ gives a matrix $M(I,J)$, where each element $m(i,j) = a(i,j)*b(i,j)$; or a product $P(T)*A(J,T)$, creates another matrix $N(J,T)$ where each element $n(j,t) = p(t)*a(j,t)$.

Chapter 4

1. This figure corresponds to 1983, which includes the effect of the nationalization of commercial banks in September 1982.

2. Weitzman and Reagan (1982).

3. Bos and Peters (1986).

4. See, for example, Jones (1982), Nellis (1986), Short (1986), and Van de Walle (1989).

5. For some time it was argued that the government could be a better manager especially in the case of firms in trouble, because in principle the problems associated with asymmetric information and of principal-agent that tended to complicate the control of managers by shareholders would not be present in public sector enterprises, to the extent that the owner and the management would be the same. However, theory and experience have proven that because the operation of parastatal entities would involve at least two groups—politicians and civil servants—the full array of complications regarding incentives and monitoring would arise. In practice, the response to this problem has been far from optimal, resulting repeatedly in excessive political intervention in the details of the managerial decision process itself, rather than the "arms-length" relationship between departments and managers that was envisioned when many of the enterprises were nationalized in the first place. For a good theoretical treatment of this topic, see Vickers and Yarrow (1988).

6. Bos and Peters (1986).

7. Pryke (1982), Forsyth (1984), Rowley and Yarrow (1981).

8. The same studies also show that when there is market power, but also a strong tendency toward a natural monopoly, there is no unequivocal evidence in favor of one type of ownership versus another, and that the final decision on whether to privatize depends on the particular characteristics of each enterprise and each industry.

9. For a more detailed explanation, see Vickers and Yarrow (1988).

10. For an excellent paper on the economics of regulation for takeovers, see Grossman and Hart (1980).

11. Besides the well-known effects of competition on resource allocation, it is also important to bear in mind that it can work as a powerful incentive mechanism to stimulate internal efficiency, as was stated originally in the studies by Hayek (1945) and Leibeinstein (1966) on X-inefficiency.

12. For a survey of these, see Vickers and Yarrow (1985); for a general theoretical treatment, see Fudenberg and Tirole (1984) and Baumol (1982).

13. Demsetz (1968).

14. The last paragraph of Article 25 says: "The law will foster and protect the economic activities carried out by private entities, and will provide with the conditions to ensure that the evolution of the private sector contributes to the economic development of the country in the terms established by this Constitution."

15. Book value, net present value of after-tax profits, market value, and liquidation value, among others.

16. In fact, at the time it became the largest "international" privatization operation through stock markets ever to take place, because the British operations happened mainly in their local domestic market.

17. Since 1983, but especially during the last four years, the aim of the public sector prices policy has been to set them at cost-recovery level without exceeding relevant international references. Thus the real prices of electricity, oil derivatives, airport services, toll roads, water, etc., were raised considerably from their 1987 levels. In this fashion, not only have the real revenues of the government been considerably reinforced, but waste of scarce goods has been discouraged. Electricity pricing has been restructured to provide firms with the possibility of choosing a peak-load pricing procedure; a national water commission was created to raise rates for water rights; the prices of oil derivatives and fertilizers have also been regionalized through charging fob prices, letting transportation costs reflect distances.

Chapter 5

1. See Sales (1991).

2. Financial savings defined as $[M(t) - M(t-1)]/GDP(t-1)$ can be decomposed in two terms, the change in the level of financial deepening: $[M(t)/GDP(t)] - [M(t-1)/GDP(t-1)]$; plus the inflation tax revenues (in a stagnant economy): $[M(t)/GDP(t)^*$ [growth rate of nominal GDP].

3. Equation 3 and the national accounts identity enter the exercise when substituted in equation 2 (see definition of AIP).

4. Hirschman (1958).

5. See, for example, Scott (1991), Lucas (1988), Romer (1989).

References

Alesina, and D. Rodrik. 1991. "The Growth Effects of Income Distribution." *CEPR Working Paper*.

Anand, Rito, and Sweder van Wijnbergen. 1988. "Inflation, External Debt and Financial Sector Reform: A Quantitative Approach to Consistent Fiscal Policy with an Application to Turkey." *NBER Working Paper* 2731:3–41.

Armendariz, Beatriz. 1990. "The Evolution of the Secondary Market Prices of the Mexican Debt (1824–1940)." Mimeo. MIT.

Aspe, Pedro, and Carlos Jarque. 1985. "Un modelo trimestral de la economía Mexicana." *El Trimestre Económico*, pp. 649–682.

Aspe, Pedro, and Javier Beristain. 1984. "The Evolution of Income Distribution Policies During the Post-Revolutionary Period in Mexico." In *The Political Economy of Income Distribution in Mexico*, edited by Pedro Aspe and Paul Sigmund. New York: Holmes and Meier.

Aspe, Pedro, and Paul Sigmund. 1984. *The Political Economy of Income Distribution in Mexico*. New York: Holmes and Meier.

Baldwin, Robert. 1989. "On the Growth Effects of 1992." *NBER Working Paper*:3–52.

Baumol, William. 1982. "Contestable Markets: An Uprising in the Theory of Industrial Structure." *American Economic Review* 72:1–15.

Blanchard, Olivier, and Stanley Fisher. 1989. "Lectures on Macro-economics." Cambridge: MIT Press.

Boreztein, E. 1989. "Debt Overhang, Credit Rationing and Invest-ment." *Journal of Development Economics*, April.

Bos, Dieter, and W. Peters. 1986. "Privatization, Efficiency and Market Structure." *Discussion Paper* A-79. Bonn University: Insti-tute of Economics.

Bruno, Michael, and Sylvia Piterman. 1988. "La Estabilización de Israel. Una reseña de dos años." In *Inflación y Estabilización*, edited by Michael Bruno et al., pp. 17–67. Mexico: Fondo de Cultura Económica.

Bruno, Michael, and Stanley Fischer. 1986. "The Inflationary Pro-cess in Israel: Shocks and Accommodation." *NBER Working Paper Series* 1483:3–48.

Buira, Ariel. 1983. "IMF financial programs and conditionality." *Journal of Development Economic* 12, 1/2:111–136.

Bulow, Jeremy, and Kenneth Rogoff. 1988. "The Buy-back Boon-dogle." *Brookings Papers on Economic Activity* 2:675–698.

Bulow, Jeremy. 1989. "Sovereign Debt Repurchases: No cure for Overhang." *NBER Working Paper* 2850:3–30.

Canavese, Alfredo, and Guido di Tella. 1988. "Estabilizar la Infla-ción o Evitar la Hiperinflación." In *Inflación y Estabilización*, edited by Michael Bruno et al., pp. 189–229. Mexico: Fondo de Cultura Economica.

Cardoso, Eliana. 1988. "El Plan Cruzado. Comentarios." In *Infla-ción y Estabilización*, edited by Michael Bruno et al., pp. 341–349. Mexico: Fondo de Cultura Economica.

Cardoso, Eliana, and Rudiger Dornbusch. 1987. "The Brazilian Tropical Plan." Mimeo: MIT.

Corden, Max, and Michael Dooley. 1989. "Issues in Debt Strategy: An Overview." In *Analytical Issues on Debt*, edited by Jacob Frankel et al. Washington: International Monetary Fund.

De Alessi, Louis. 1977. "Ownership and Peak Load Pricing in the Electric Power Industry." *Quarterly Review of Economics and Business* 17:7–26.

Demsetz, H. 1968. "Why Regulate Utilities?." *Journal of Law and Economics*, March.

Deppler, W., and J. Williamson. 1987. "Capital Flight: Concepts, Measurements and Issues." In *Staff Studies for the World Economic Outlook*. Washington, D.C.: International Monetary Fund.

Díaz Alejandro, Carlos. 1981. "Southern Cone Stabilization Plans." In *Economic Stabilization in Developing Countries*, edited by William Cline and Sidney Weintraub et al. Washington, D.C.: The Brookings Institution.

Díaz Alejandro, Carlos. 1985. "Good Bye Financial Repression, Hello Financial Crash." *Journal of Development Economics* 19, nos. 1/2:1–24.

Dixit, Avinash. 1980. "The Role of Investment in Entry-Deterrence." *Economic Journal* 90:95–106.

Dooley, M. 1988. "Self Financed Buy-backs and Asset Exchanges." *IMF Staff papers*.

Dornbusch, Rudiger. 1988. "Notes on Credibility and Stabilization." *NBER Working Paper* 2790, 1–18.

Dornbusch, Rudiger, and Alejandro Reynoso. 1989. "Financial Factors in Economic Development," *American Economic Review, Papers and Proceedings* 7:204–214.

Dornbusch, Rudiger, and Alejandro Reynoso. 1990. "Note on the Dynamics of Dollarization: A logistic infection model for Mexico and Peru." Mimeo: MIT.

Dornbusch, Rudiger, and Mario Henrique Simonsen. 1987. "Inflation, Stabilization with Incomes Policy Support." New York: El Grupo de los Treinta.

Eaton, J. 1987. "Public Debt Guarantees and Private Capital Flight." *The World Bank Economic Review* 1, no. 3:377–395.

Eaton, Jonathan, and Mark Gersovitz. 1981. "Debt with Potential Repudiation: Theoretical and Empirical Analysis." *Review of Economic Studies* 48:289–309.

Eaton, Jonathan, Mark Gersovitz, and J. Stiglitz. 1986. "The Pure Theory of Country Risk." *European Economic Review* 30:481–514.

Eichengreen, Barry, and R. Portes. 1986. "Debt and Default in the 1930's: Causes and Consequences." *European Economic Review* 30:599–640.

Fanelli, José María, and José Luis Machinea. 1988. "Control de la Hiperinflación: El caso del Plan Austral." In *Inflación y Estabilización*, edited by Michael Bruno et al. Mexico: Fondo de Cultura Economica.

Feldstein, Martin, and Horioka, Charles. 1979. "On the Determinants of Savings and Investment." Mimeo: Harvard University.

Fischer, Stanley. 1977. "Wage Indexation and Macroeconomic Stability." *Carnegie Rochester Series on Public Policy*.

Fischer, Stanley. 1979. "Dynamic Inconsistency, Cooperation and the Benevolent Disembling Government." Mimeo: MIT.

Fischer, Stanley. 1988. "Seigniorage and the Case for a National Money" ed. at *Indexing, Inflation and Economic Policy*. Cambridge: MIT Press.

Fishlow, Albert. (1986) "Lessons from the Past: Capital Markets during the 19th Century and the Interwar Period." In *The Politics of International Debt*, edited by Miles Kahler. Ithaca New York: Cornell University Press.

Forsyth, P. J. 1984. "Airlines and Airports: Privatisation, Regulation and Competition." *Fiscal Studies*.

Friedman, Milton. 1968. "The Role of Monetary Policy." *American Economic Review* 58, no. 1:1–17.

Froot, Kenneth. 1988. "Buybacks, Exit Bonds and the Optimality of Debt and Liquidity Relief." *NBER Working Paper* 2675:1–33.

Fry, Maxwell. 1988. "Money Interest and Banking in Economic Development." Baltimore: Johns Hopkins University Press, pp. 477–525.

Fudenberg, Drew, and Jean Tirole. 1984. "The Fat-Cat Effect, the Puppy-Dog Ploy, and the Lean and Hungry Look." *American Economic Review, Papers and Proceedings* 74, no. 2:361–368.

Gil, Francisco. 1984. "The Incidence of Taxes in Mexico: A Before and After Comparison." In *The Political Economy of Income Distribution in Mexico*, edited by Pedro Aspe and Paul Sigmund, pp. 59–98. New York: Holmes and Meier.

Grossman, Sanford, and Oliver Hart. 1980. "Takeover Bids, the Free Rider Problem and the Theory of the Corporation." *Bell Journal of Economics* 2:42–64.

Hayek, Friedrich August. 1945. "The Use of Knowledge in Society." *American Economic Review* 35:519–530.

Helpman, Elhanan. 1987. "Price Controls, Economic Efficiency and Market Structure." Mimeo: MIT.

Hernández, Silvia, and Alejandro Reynoso. 1990. "Expectativas y Estabilización. Un Modelo Bayesiano de Inflación Inercial para el Pacto de Solidaridad Económica en México." Mimeo: Secretaria de Hacienda y Credito Publico.

Hierro, Jorge. 1988. "Financial Liberalization and Inflation." Mimeo: MIT.

Hirschman, Albert. 1958. "The Strategy of Economic Development." New Haven: Yale University Press.

Jones, Leroy. 1982. "Public Enterprise in Less Developed Countries." Cambridge: Cambridge University Press.

Kaldor, Nicholas, 1973. "Las Reformas al Sistema en Mexico" in Solis, Leopoldo *La economía Mexicana: Política y Desarrollo*. Mexico: Fondo de Cultura Economica.

Kindleberger, Charles. 1971. "The World in Depression (1929–1939)." Berkeley: University of California Press.

Kroll, H. 1991. "Monopoly and Transition to the Market." Soviet Economy.

Krueger, Anne. 1978. "Foreign Trade Regimes and Economic Development: Liberalization Attempts and Consequences." Cambridge: NBER.

Krugman, Paul. 1979. "A Model of Balance of Payments Crisis," *Journal of Money Credit and Banking* 11, no. 3:311–325.

Krugman, Paul. 1985. "International Debt Strategies in an Uncertain World." In *The International Debt and the Developing Countries*, edited by G. Smith and John Cuddington. A World Bank Symposium.

Krugman, Paul. 1989. "Market Based Debt Reduction Schemes." *NBER Working Paper*.

Krugman, Paul, and Lance Taylor. 1978. "The Contractionary Effects of a Devaluation." *Journal of International Economics* 8, no. 3:445–456.

Lanyi, A., and R. Scorogulu. 1983. "Interest Rate Policies in Developing Countries." *International Monetary Fund Occasional Papers* 22.

Leibeinstein, Harvey. 1966. "Allocative Efficiency versus X-Efficiency." *American Economic Review* 56:392–415.

Lucas, Robert. 1973. "Some International Evidence on Output-Inflation Trade-Offs." *American Economic Review* 63, no. 3:326–334.

Lucas, Robert. 1988. "On the Mechanism of Economic Development." *Journal of Monetary Economics* 22:3–42.

McKinnon, Ronald. 1973. "Money and Capital in Economic Development." Washington, D.C.: The Brookings Institution.

McKinnon, Ronald, and Donald Mathieson. 1981. "How to Manage a Repressed Economy," *Princeton Essays in International Finance* 145:1–30.

Marglin, Stephen. 1984. "Growth, Distribution and Prices." Cambridge: Harvard University Press.

Miller, V. 1989. "Bond Maturity and Inflation Uncertainty: The Case of Mexico." Unpublished Thesis: MIT.

Millward, Robert. 1982. "The Comparative Performance of Public and Private Ownership." In *The Mixed Economy*, edited by Eric Roll, pp. 58–93. London: Macmillan Press.

Modiano, Eduardo. 1988. "El Primer Intento del Cruzado." In *Inflación y Estabilización*, edited by Michael Bruno et al. Mexico: Fondo de Cultura Economica.

Nellis, J. 1986. "Public Enterprises in Sub-Saharan Africa." Washington, D.C.: The World Bank.

Peltzman, S. 1971. "Pricing in Public and Private Enterprises: Electric Utilities in the United States." *Journal of Law and Economics* 14, no. 1:109–148.

Polak, J. 1957. "Monetary Analysis of Income Formation and Payments Problems." *IMF Staff Papers*.

Porter, Michael. 1990. "The Competitive Advantage of Nations." New York: The Free Press.

Pryke, R. 1982. "The Comparative Performance of Public and Private Enterprise." *Fiscal Studies*.

Ramirez, C. 1985. "Currency Substitution in Argentina, Mexico and Uruguay." *IMF Staff Papers*.

Reynoso, Alejandro. 1989. "Essays on the Macroeconomic Effects of Monetary Reforms, Price Controls and Financial Repression." Unpublished Ph.D dissertation: MIT.

Reynoso, Alejandro. 1988. "When Financial Regulation becomes Financial Repression: A Look at the Case of Mexico (1940–1985)." Mimeo: MIT.

Reynoso, Alejandro. 1990. "Inflación y Estructura Económica." Mimeo: Secretaria de Hacienda y CreditoPublico.

Romer, Paul. 1989. "Increasing Returns and New Developments in the Theory of Growth." *NBER Working Paper* 3098:1–37.

Sachs, Jeffrey. 1983. "Theoretical Issues in International Borrowing." *NBER Working Paper* 1189:1–48.

Sachs, Jeffrey. 1989. "Conditionality, Debt Relief and the Developing Country Debt Crisis," Mimeo: Harvard University.

Sales, Carlos. 1991. "On the Determinants of Foreign Investment in Mexico." Mimeo: Harvard University.

Scott, M. 1991. "A New View of Economic Growth." *World Bank Discussion Papers* 131. Washington, D.C.: World Bank.

Short, R. P. 1986. "The Role of Public Enterprises: An International Statistical Comparison." In *Public Enterprise in Mixed Economies: Some Macroeconomic Aspects*, edited by Floyd et al. Washington: International Monetary Fund.

Solís, Leopoldo. 1973. "La Economia Mexicana. Politica y Desarrollo." Mexico: Fondo de Cultura Economica.

Solís, Leopoldo, and Dwight S. Brothers. 1970. "The Mexican Financial System." New Haven: Yale University Press.

Solís, Leopoldo. 1981. "Economic Policy Reform in Mexico: A Case Study for Developing Countries." New York: Pergamon Press.

Solís, Leopoldo, and Ernesto Zedillo. 1985. "The Foreign Debt of Mexico." In *The International Debt and the Developing Countries*, edited by G. Smith and J. Cuddington. A World Bank Symposium.

Taylor, J. 1980. "Aggregate Dynamics and Staggered Contracts." *Journal of Political Economy*.

Taylor, J. 1979. "Estimation and Control of a Macroeconomic Model with Rational Expectations." *Econometrica* 47-5:1267–1286.

Taylor, Lance. 1983. "Structuralist Macroeconomics. Applicable Models for the Third World." New York: Basic Books.

Tellez, Luis. 1986. "Essays on the History of Mexico's Debt." Unpublished Ph.D Thesis: MIT.

Tenkate, A. 1990. "Proteccionismo versus Apertura Comercial." Mimeo: Universidad Nacional de Costa Rica.

Thompson, W., and K. Robbie. 1991. "Privatization via Management and Employee Buyouts."

Van de Walle, Nicholas. 1989. "Privatization in Developing Countries: A Review of the Issues." *World Development* 17, no. 5:601–615.

Van Wijnbergen, S. 1985. "Macro-economic Effects of Changes in Bank Interest Rates: Simulation Results for South Korea," *Journal of Development Economics* 18, nos. 2–3: 541–554.

Van Wijnbergen, S. 1988. "Inflation, Balance of Payments Crises, and Public Sector Deficits." In *Economic Effects of the Government Budget*, edited by Helpman, Elhanan et al. Cambridge: MIT Press.

Vickers, John, and G. Yarrow. 1985. "Privatization and Natural Monopolies." London: Public Policy Centre.

Vickers, John, and G. Yarrow. 1988. "Privatization." Cambridge: MIT Press.

Weitzman, Martin, and Patricia Reagan. 1982. "Asymmetries in Price and Quantity Adjustment by the Competitive Firm." *Journal of Economic Theory* 27, no. 2:410–420.

Whalley, John. 1989. "Recent Trade Liberalization in the Developing World: What is Behind It and Where is It Headed?. *NBER Working Paper* 3057:1–45.

World Bank. 1991. *The World Development Report*. Washington, D.C.

Zedillo, Ernesto. 1981. "External Public Indebtedness in Mexico: Recent History and Future Oil Bounded Optimal Growth." Unpublished Ph.D dissertation: Yale University.

Index